Rings of Truth
The First Fountain of Fantasy
The 10th Fountain
(Forces of Faith Version)

Robert Koyich

DEDICATION

To my lovestone, even if I didn't yet know who you are,
here we are, orbiting around the very same star.

CONTENTS

REFORMATION

Rings of Truth is the first Fountain of Fantasy. I wrote this book to expand my ability and to envision the future, and as the Fountains continue the process of my work, it's a way to write my dreams into life. I also acknowledge the struggles within; fantasies can start as a wish. With vision, work, and clarity, our souls and spirits meld to be more real.

"We author our own life."

What I'm doing stems from wishes and hope. What I've done may ignite a spark in the tinder of mind, yet sometimes we can control the flame. Fire can be helpful yet dualistic, and imagine what we can do if we learn to manage and share love like we have the power of light.

I must be careful not to become rampant and torch the fields, though some gardens may appreciate the winter shroud of snow and allow the bulbs of Spring to bloom. It's my responsibility to use my powers to help and heal our world. I remember not all people want to do good, though. I desire to be a plus one and not a negative one, so those who read these books are Earthlings who have an impulse to give.

The first Fountains cast foundational blocks of text. Later, *Shards of My Soul* called for completion. The base text of this book started before Shards' release, and I felt impelled to start this text and move into the future. If the Fountains cover the dreams, wishes, and visions held, then perhaps we should get into the thick of this.

I want to tell you what I want. I also recommend you tell others what *you* want. When we know our desires, it's then we can work towards them. If yesterday affects faith, we build fortitude, and when we hold the courage to develop fantasies into realities, we may flourish. Perhaps my wishes resolve to become more faithful.

Previously, I've written prayers and repentance to God with Christian overtones. An alternative form of faith is having faith in ourselves. When people perform work for someone other than themselves, it can bolster their confidence, grit, and determination. I work for Earth, even if God may not like that.

For who do we want to provide? For whom shall we work? What can I do to offer more than I have already, and do I believe I can do more? Is the desire to work for how it feels to thrive? Do we want to have a more positive effect? Or is it about earning more money? We must clarify why we're doing what we do.

For me, it's all three things; the feeling of earning, doing something worthwhile, and because I like and love having money and sharing ideas. Are you happy doing what you're doing? If not, then what could you do differently? I don't know your circumstances, though I intuit I can do much more to guide our lives into better situations.

Some people believe they can't do anything different than they're already doing. It takes effort, dedication, and perseverance to be okay to do what we need to do to be where we want to be. My Mom would say, we can't just wave a magic wand and wish for things to be better; we can, though, make positive choices to adjust our futures. If we want a better future, we must clearly define what that means to us.

I've lacked gumption and clarity about what I want, though I learn why. Generalized wishes of prosperity, happiness, and success need to hone into specifics. What is wealth, joy, and success for you or me? What if the things we want and do contradict those definitions? I know I've not yet produced fantastic results, yet setting future goals adjust behaviours.

I've talked about the topic of smoking in previous books, and if we look at people who are prosperous, happy, and successful, how many of them have you seen smoking a cigarette? It seems contradictive for me to burn while also wanting longevity. I'd like to develop to be more future sighted and optimistic, and though I can't predict the future, I want to envision and *plan* for longevity. There are habits I need to break, many practices I need to develop, and through incremental improvement, legitimate breakthroughs can leap us forward.

One thing I strongly recommend is purchasing and reading books that expand you, your world, your mind, and your abilities. If you're reading *this* book, you're presumably a reader, though are you reading to escape reality, look into mine, or because you earnestly want to learn something?

If you're looking for specific, focused skills, directives, or purpose, try Brendon Burchard's book *High-Performance Habits*. Brendon adds knowledge about how to adjust attitudes and behaviours, and depending on your reasons for reading, his book may be the right book to read.

I want to write creative ideas, recommend insights, and procure soulful imagination. My books use the first-person pronoun a lot, and I'm writing to tell you things that may be valuable or helpful for you too.

It was 11:31 PM on Saturday, February 9th, 2019, when I started writing this. My classic caffeine and late-night writing sessions were in action, and I had watched two YouTube videos. One was about how much writers earn, and another was advice about authorship from eleven successful authors.

It was 11:49 PM Wednesday, August 14th, 2019, when I started the first revision. The late nights alone and multi-year incubation process is the sandwich I eat that Elizabeth Gilbert spoke of in one of the YouTube videos. Does another chew on my infidelity instead?

Since this is the first Fountain of Fantasy, please let me draw the threads from the loom. Though meeting Natalie is a bucket-list item I hold, competing on Survivor is too. It's ultra-ridiculous to think of doing so, yet both are worthwhile experiences. I also surprise myself and our community by gathering a few hundred dollars in pledges in the next year.

I found summer 2019 a profitable season for building our future. The snow barely fell the previous winter when I was supposed to shovel snow, though a different job, landscaping, surfaced. I work for Sovereign Landscaping as of Fall 2018, and Brad, my boss, has been fantastic. I earn to clear my debts, set aside savings, and hopefully afford a car.

My Dad and his wife are glad I'm working too. They flew out for a trip, and I admit I felt a bit envious. I want to go on flights also, though the main thing I'm missing (other than travel money) when I typed this was a travelling companion. I've not met a gal who can make trips overseas with me to visit and feel the air in other nations.

It'll be drastically different living with a gal again, though amazingly worth it. It's been a long time since having a girlfriend, and other than Rizz at Simon Fraser University in 1998, I've not lived with a female companion.

The process of hooking up with a gal is a tricky one for me. I've been out of the dating game a long while, and I've not slept in the same bed with someone (other than my cats) since going out with a gal in 2004-2005. My bed holds an empty spot for a real lovestone, though I need to absolutely trust her.

I have concerns about my next girlfriend and my up-to-now long-term solo mission. I'm concerned I'll embarrass myself if we get naked together! I've not even kissed a girl since 2015, though the species differential allows me to snuggle my cat and give him love; the gender bias I hold for physical contact doesn't apply to cats. I would have preferred a female cat as a pet, though trusting in the process of fate and destiny, I adopted Zeus.

The first Fountain, *Finding Natalie*, had a chapter written to a friend nicknamed Chandra. She and I talk quite well, though we didn't hook up as a couple. I wrote a chapter to her in angst, and later she asked I don't include the section in the final version of the book. I also wrote to another female friend codenamed Elspeth in *Fields of Formation*, though that chapter stayed as part of the book *The Sands of Yesterday*.

Both Chandra and Elspeth are quite different, though both are liked and appreciated. Chandra will speak on the phone, visits, and values me as a friend, and though Elspeth too may value me as a friend, she rarely responds to messages and barely ever calls.

I only have a few friends and know only a few people. Because I'm not emotionally close to many and I don't have a best friend, I don't have a lot of friends I can call. I'd like more female friends, and when I want to talk, there are some I want to call, though don't hear from them. What I want to find are more positive mutually reciprocal relationships.

I'd also like a primary girlfriend. By having only a few contacts, I've not had much communication, yet I learn how to converse better. With women, my history has been tainted; I've liked some gals a lot and then creep-showed, over-obsessed, or hadn't fully committed. I held myself away from romance when I fixated on Natalie, and that could be a reason gals stayed away for a few years.

Now that I know Natalie's probably not good for me, I'm more open to a real relationship. It's almost like I'm on the rebound from divorce without ever being in the same room as my 'ex'-wife. And where am I going? If Natalie and the Seed Fund were life-long objectives and I released her, I've not stepped up with a personal mission. It leads to building a home, and I wonder how to form my prayers of penance for holding the desires I've claimed.

If we find our wishes of heart and what we want aren't perfect things for us, can we take requests back? If to reform wants and desires, can we discover what our attractions are? Perhaps we do learn what is good or right for each other and build that way.

What's best for me leads to quitting smoking, yet I've held onto that crutch with a terrible resolve. One night early Spring 2019, I went to bed wishing to be alive fifty years from now. I should remember I want that more often. I desire to feel inspired, active and engaged and working on things that matter to me, and if true, I best work on our relationships.

5

Crucially, I want to earn my way and start gathering. I waffled on pledge gathering when I wrote this, though the bizarre calling keeps hounding me. I've felt frustrated and agitated and also have felt obsessed energetically. I've not always been passionate about gathering pledges, even for myself.

A reformation finds undercurrents leveraging activities for my benefit. Since I want to earn my way in life, maybe I should connect with others who also want to make, create, or discover their ideas and path.

The homelessness and street focus push and pull me in different ways. I want to find ways of relieving situations of lack, though I'm concerned if I don't devote myself entirely to the program, people will get mad at me. I don't want to quit or give up, yet I want to be free to act for my benefit too. I love having the luxury of only earning for myself, yet I'd like to share more. The kicker is the question; what if I can do both?

I don't want to throw money or crumbs at people and call them nuggets of gold either, though. The money gathered from book sales up to August 2019 isn't even close to the $800 it costs to cover a month or rent for a decent home. If my vision board says I earn enough money to how a thousand people from book sales, how can I make sales significant enough to do so?

Up to when I typed this, it seems like the market doesn't want my books or music. Even giving away freebies to people hasn't generated much interest in my creations. If I've shared a hundred or two hundred books, and people like them, there haven't yet been additional sales up to this release. Even if I was paid for each copy given, it's not big money big prizes. If my creative work is to house people, we'll need to sell thousands of books.

Is this Fountain gathering more of the components of freedom? Tracking how we can find Freedom Solutions via legitimate pathways reminds me free money is helpful. It's even more gratifying to earn from personal efforts and be the one to provide that money.

I've not advertised the Providing Point program, and I'm not fond of fundraising. Instead, the program develops naturally by sharing books with people and talking about the issues and goals openly. I've done that since Fountain four, and though I've put in the time, effort, and energy into these books, and, passively, Providing Point stands. I haven't been push promoting and may not.

That may be why there's been a drastic lack of results. Yet an impulsion to create and talk about this program call me into being okay in the moment of now. If we focus only on ourselves and our gain, or demean others to get the upper hand, that's not the pathway of how I want to be.

I'm on a pathway of care, inclusion, and respect with others who develop myself, my work, and my intents. I hope too that I'm creating ideas beneficial for encouraging positive channels of activity. I'm committed to the process of love and life and endure the slings and narrows of the view to how we remember I'm explicitly not You.

For those that are Christian and looking for Jesus, I can clearly and succinctly tell and remind you: I'm not the man you are looking for! I'm not a Messiah, God, or omniscient deity; I'm just a kid on Earth who's not learned how to 'adult' so well. I also seem to refuse to quit without getting my hands, heart, and soul deep in the work required.

For those that are part of the consect and street community, I know I'm not hardcore or street. I have concern, empathy, regard, and reverence for some of you, yet I know I'm not living the lives you are either. I may be pushing my mind, my work, and my ideas into areas of your turf and territory, yet I'm not seeking to uproot you. I'm still just one person who wants to find a sure path and be okay.

I've wanted to shift from talking about providing for others and become self-reliant by activating my heart, and I must earn my living instead of relying on guilt offerings. Soliciting pledges for Share and Care cards can keep a path to shared prosperity, yet I also must allow myself to thrive and succeed with this work too. We all have something to gain from these books.

I keep www.Patreon.com/Introversial open for accepting pledges and abide by my promised contribution commitments from previous Fountains. The money earned from Fountains sales shall go to the causes they're meant for, and I also forge new activities, connections, and behaviours; to allow myself my wife, our home, and a family of many that include our friends.

Earth *is* a shared planet, and if we each can secure how to give and help achieve our successes, we all may live more brilliantly, vibrantly, and with a more explicit manifestation of peace, love, unity, and respect.

ACROSS AN OCEAN

I'd been reading the book *The 4-Hour Workweek* by Tim Ferris. The book is not about slacking off, sleeping away the days, or watching Netflix as a professional hobby. The book has tactical ideas about how to develop a life we can love instead of being trapped in full-time mind-numbing work.

For those who are waiting for retirement twenty to forty years later, Tim shares some valuable information about how to actualize more of your heart's yearnings, now. Tim's book also shares how to start up an online company with the support of automation and outsourcing to generate a substantial income.

When I first typed this, I didn't know what to focus on to earn my pay. I knew, though, some Freedom Solution numbers. If I can sell fifty units of 'me' a day, I can live luxuriously, afford to travel, and also have money to share. A question is, "how I shall sell that many units a day?" What can I do when I do sell that many units a day?

I think of travel, and the first place that comes to mind is usually Italy. I went to Italy in 2016, and I want to visit there again, partly because of the language. Italian is my second most fluent language, so I see going to that country as more logical. Although it's scary, I want to go for a few weeks and wonder about going for a three-month mini-retirement.

Natalie is also part of Italy and the title of this chapter. I've not been thinking so much about her recently, though there's always a corner of my heart kept for her. I don't yet know who receives my entire love, and though Zeus is a kind pet, I need a female companion. I can't and mustn't hold myself away from a real relationship by holding onto an idea of someone I fell for two decades ago. I want to find *my* lovestone and be *her* man.

The wish is I find my love and travel with her. It's not

9

going to happen magically by just wishing; I need to put in the effort to find love. That's what I've been reading in books; we need to work, plan, and cultivate actions to allow us to have the lives we want to live and love.

I remind myself relationships are a high value of mine. Since my books are 'all-about-me,' then the target audience for my books are not specific niches, yet seemingly those interested in me. I write recommendations and ideas, though I need to heed my advice too. "Rob! Make some new friends and just be a super-decent person!"

A friend I labelled Gideon and Jeskai cues me to remember I've neglected to contact people I like and love. Writing *is* solitary, and though I can bring a laptop to Italy to write more, I think I first need to work for a community and a friend circle here in town.

There's a friend that I've complained about a lot. The reluctance of interacting so much with them is how I get overly triggered by their behaviours and actions. I've thought if I've felt so negative about them that I should just avoid contact.

If we get pissed off and angry and are meant to accept that's part of how we can be, then what and where is the right outlet for displeasure? Many people tell us not to complain, yet when frustrated and needing to vent, I also don't want to trap the bad feelings in my heart or psyche; that could be damaging.

I remember a technique and experience from *PD Seminars: Haven by the Sea.* The experience is called a Vesuvius. It's not Pompeii, a place to visit, though instead is an exercise that's a healthy way to release anger.

A Vesuvius is a group activity where a participant is given space, safety, and freedom to purge their anger. With the respected boundary of the person staying in a defined and separate area from the audience, they can yell, scream, stomp, curse, and cuss out all of their anger. The objective is to release the entirety of the participant's displeasure and purge all the secretly held feelings. A key point is that people are present to witness the session and that the person performing the Vesusvisu is seen and heard. The audience helps support the participant by observing the event.

I've wanted to have a Vesuvius. I've felt dramatic amounts of agitation and have been quite vulgar and reactive to people who deserve kindness. Some of it may be from hating myself and not achieving much; a generalized frustration, and I've not been happy. Writing is therapeutic, though my anger is more like wanting to smash the keyboard and destroy things instead of focusing and forming eloquent words for an audience.

Who am I writing for precisely? I'm unfocused with the book's direction and have written outwards generally again. I needn't just hone what I'm doing, though I must atone for what I've done. In one way, giving the proceeds from the books can tend to the causes people are helping by buying a copy, yet is that a guilt offering?

The night I wrote this part of the first draft, I gave $11.80 from two copies of *Fragments of Intent* to Ann Davis and $3.36 to Ruth and Naomi's from the sale of one copy of *Open to Fate*. If I'm going to write books and create seed fields that flourish, I need to know who I'm writing to and for.

We can craft our words for specific audiences, yet I often don't know who I'm telling. Some authors write a lot on a topic focused on a niche audience and can hone their marketing in line. Some authors write books in different genres to reach a wider audience, though I've taken a different path with authorship, and it's not one I'd recommend.

A local entrepreneur named Dave commented on how he thinks I'm "trying to boil the ocean." Dave recommended I focus on only one thing. When I told my Dad what Dave suggested, I knew a question I couldn't answer was, "focus on what?"

If I'm to write to a broad audience (the ocean), then how could I bubble up any interest. If I write for a small few people that want to read what I write (a pot), that could be even better and easier to raise some steam. Steam engines are quite useful, though what about Hydrogen fuel cells?

We can get clear and concise with our message or craft, yet still, be like unfocused light. I may need to hone and focus like a laser. I've received lots of advice and read some great books, though the information isn't enough. I need to activate my ideas and also actualize my desires.

What we *try* to do or *think* to do isn't often what we *actually* do. I've *wanted* to write books that people want to read and *think* I've made some good tracks, yet the market results up to September 2019 show that neither my books nor music have a demand.

If my Facebook friends haven't yet seen a post about "please ask me for a book" or "check out my Bandcamp page," they aren't so active on Facebook. I remember that just because I make a post on Facebook, it doesn't mean every friend sees it, yet with the number posts I've made (and the many personal messages) asking people to read a book or play some music, I bet that most of my contacts know.

If we're creators, we must remember that Facebook, Instagram, or Twitter are often platforms where we can gather readers, listeners or fans. That said, just because we've made something, it doesn't mean people will give us attention, time, or money to process it.

Push marketing can, like in my doing, be like spam and push many genuine friends away from interacting. There are billions of humans on this planet, though our friend circles mayhap should be for friends and not soliciting sales.

That said, if our products or services are valuable, there's more of a likelihood someone we know will purchase. If we're to succeed in selling our work, then we must perform excellent work and find our viable audience. I may have flooded my local contacts with requests to play my music, buy or read my books, or give a pledge.

Dave's advice about focusing narrowed me into knowing I don't want an NGO to be my main job. Music is something I enjoy, and even with that, I'm very passive. Books can more accurately convey and hone my intents, yet people aren't yet so interested in supporting. I want to share valuable information, I like shifting into rhyme mode sometimes, and I also love sharing resources. Knowing those three things (books, music, and giving) and why I want to do them find me to admit something; I prefer to write compared to making tracks or fundraising.

If you have many desires or options, you know it may be challenging to focus and hone in on one thing. I also hope you know that when you reach your perfect moments of flow, that you can acknowledge you like or love those things. The trick about being a profitable creative is also knowing what we can sell and creating that.

Some people have wanted to be mainstream artists to make the big paycheck, yet the sacrifices are often not enjoyable. Being a best-selling author can lure and generate fame, yet if you don't want to be famous, it's a different trip. With my past events, I've thought it dangerous to be overly known, yet where I shift to is healing my trauma and learning valuable skills and information and sharing it.

I started with an inversed focus on Natalie with the Fountains, yet she wasn't receptive to it. Upon reflection, I scattered outwards with fragments and then fell upon the shores of time amongst all the other grains of sand that wanted to be a pearl with her.

If Natalie's rooted in the ocean - in her shell keeping shut to prevent invaders - then how could a lonesome grain of sand like me get tripped into her world? I honestly don't know, though, in some ways, the years of agitation have formed these books stringing together one after the next. If you have only one pearl, though, how can you make an entire necklace?

Returning from the metaphors, how do I want this book to be valuable? If I created the first books with a different intent in each, then where are we in the journey?

Few would want to buy someone's journal unless it was

an exciting or famous person. I have an idea people know who I am, yet perhaps I'm not so impressive. Some want solutions to their problems, not to read a babbler, so if I don't narrow down the purpose of what questions I'm solving, then how can I direct answers?

If you want to write a book, be sure to start it. If you're going to make music for the pure sake of enjoyment, do so. It's best to know why you're doing what you do, and if you'd like to sell books or music, realize it's a different process.

I planned to sell thousands of copies, meet Natalie, and house people by writing books, so I wrote them. I didn't think about commercial viability, though, and we need to know who I'm creating for. What do people want to know? I've not entirely tended my answer to that.

A commercially successful focus is much different than gratifying creative expression. Is your work for business prosperity or personal satisfaction? If I'm to focus on my audience to increase potential sales, then I shouldn't write so much about myself unless others want to read about me.

The idea is I can still succeed very well with creation and relationships without earning money. The trick is I'd like to make a substantial income too. Some may be exceptionally fortunate with sales and profits and still feel miserable, so what is the cost of money? I prefer to ask ourselves, "What can we do with the money?"

If people have a clear intent to share their resources with people who need things, what happens when those people earn more? If someone has correct ethics, real purpose, and actively abides by those ethics and mission, shouldn't we allow them more to activate good things in the future?

My calls to action have been few. Copywriting (not copyrighting) tells us that when we craft advertisements that we need to consider what the customer's wants are and talk about benefits. Copywriting applies to how words can be crafted to solicit action. Seth Godin writes about how marketing is not so much *what can I sell* and *for how much* yet instead suggests that marketing should be "to make things better [and] to cause a change you'd like to see in the world."

Holding that statement, then each of my books is marketing dreams, faith, hope, and love. I'd love for our world to find each to have enough to provide more than just the basic needs of people. I want us to expand to see people achieve their dreams.

If the best things we can do are good for us, good for others, and good for the world, then I think finding my lovestone could be a pretty good thing. It may not be I'm ready yet to be a loyal parent or husband at this point, yet I know a real girlfriend would be fantastic.

When working with a partner or mate towards broad objectives, I've heard and read it's a marvellous thing. The principle of Masterminding edges me forward a bit further to have a partner to plot and plan great things. From my experience, I know working solitarily and without counsel isn't enough.

If I were to retake the past twenty years knowing Natalie was a complete no-go from the start, I'd have lived much differently. Since I didn't, I must make the best of my situation and parameters and find my path. A broad stroke over the canvas can help start the work, yet the fine details painted later often are what refine art into a masterpiece.

Natalie splashed all over my canvas in 1998, though instead of throwing the work away, my soul accepted her as part of myself. I try to find a way of painting a picture worthwhile of sharing with the world instead of tossing the piece into the bin. I may not admit she knows me these years later, though, with a deep breath, I realize it was I who betrayed her.

It may be because I'm an obsessed Muppet dangling on Geppetto's strings, yet we'll make a real boy out of this kid; one whose nose has grown so far out there that Saturn might have to send its rings back to the printer for another batch.

When and if I marry someone, I want to get it right the first time. First things first, though; find the gal who wants to live with Zeus and me, even if we're not there yet.

BLOCKING TIME

My pathway to profitable authorship has been messy. The first three to four books were atrocious structurally and grammatically, though, by the release of the sixth Fountain book, I'd learned a lot. I've improved and refined my writing process.

When I purchased the professional version of Grammarly, I went back to the previous Fountains and distilled them. I cleaned up the books, and the result is, hopefully, clean water. I've not yet had any of my books professionally edited, yet have learned heaps since l started writing on my own.

A challenge with writing a book is editing services cost a lot. Editors.ca says we could expect to pay up to $60 an hour for a freelance editor whose a professional in our industry. Some startup writers may not even have the $60 for food, let alone an editor, though if you don't have the cash to spend, and are aiming for a profitable authorship path, you'll need to learn how to edit.

In the 5th Fountain in 2017, I got overconfident in my editing skills. I was levelling up and thought I was getting excellent, though after getting Grammarly, I found a vast number of mistakes. There were hundreds of errors in what I thought was a finished document. If you can't afford an editor, make sure you get the program to help you.

A premium version of Grammarly costs $139.95, though if you're concerned about cost, they often offer a promotion where you can purchase with a 45%-55% discount. The program is *entirely* worth it, and if you assess the quality of my work, it's the result of a few years of learning and a professional subscription.

I like to read books about personal development and planning for success. I may not soak in and activate all of the vital information, yet I learn a lot. By being a writer, I've learned to appreciate good writing, and I know writing well with valuable information is a stellar combo.

My first books are all about me and what I want to do, yet recently I've thought about writing for those who want to write too. It makes sense with how other authors find their niches; by having an interest and then diving into the topic and gaining trial and error experience working in that field.

I also like the idea of sharing big ideas, yet the way I approached Providing Point and my books was backwards. I looked at how much I could gather from a price, not how much value I can provide to be worthy of a purchase.

If money is the motivator, it can draw us to work, yet if we write for a cause and with a purpose, it can assist belief in the worth of our work. We need to value our work for how much another may benefit from it; more than just our gain. If we create only for profit, there is less value in what we can create, and if you're profit-focused and see few results, it can allure one to give up or quit.

I write partly from obsession, and also to earn a living. My first book was to get the girl, though it shifted to making money later on. I now write to share myself and my ideas and also aspire to convey worth and value. To allow earnings, I've been the cart before the horse with some things, and I don't mean to be incongruent.

When starting to share our work with the world, there's an impulse to want anyone and everyone to read or buy a copy. I thought sharing free books would encourage people to purchase others in the series, thereby selling more. After two years of sharing books, though, I've not sold so many.

Perhaps I need to rethink my plots and plans. It may not be great to give free copies if seeking monetary gain. If someone would buy a copy, and they receive one for free, then there's zero chance of them buying that book. Writing a series can encourage cross-sales, though if starting with just one book, I'm not clear sharing free copies is the best. If starting by aiming for local success, it can be easy to flood the market with as few as a hundred copies.

Another challenge about selling books is that the sale is more than a monetary transaction. If a person buys a book, they have to be interested in the book, and they also (if they read the book) are giving us their time to process our words. If you're to write a book, create a quality book that's worth both the time, money, and effort to read. The more people that buy a book *and* love what they read, the higher chance there is for referrals.

The ultra-successful books are sometimes marketed on *who* wrote the book, yet there are others written by previously unknown people that have not just written an excellent book, though they have also sold well. If you can create quality text combined with valuable information, there is a challenge of exposure, yet think of virality with books too. Some books become phenomenally successful because they entrance their audience and form a following.

If you've read my books, you've seen me refer to some influential books and authors. They create great things, so I'm compelled to share them. At the point of forming this book, I'd not had a massive influence, yet the trickling of other's liquid gold fuses in like Kintsugi into my work. If you are to write books, find the golden truths, wisdom, and guides that fuel yourself. Find ways to pass on their knowledge to your potential readers, but be sure to give the originators credit.

I think everyone should write a book. If you don't know what to write about, it is a challenge you can overcome. Freewriting on a computer or in a notebook is a great way to start. Just write out anything that comes to mind and don't stop; force your keys to move the cursor along the screen or pen across the pad. You can also use the tactic of choosing one person to write to and tell them what you want them to know.

Who am I telling? What am I telling them? Why do they need to know? By writing slowly and intentionally craft the words to be just for them. Freewriting activates our ability to produce words and ideas, though focusing on one person can dredge up feelings and deepen intent.

I can't give great advice about fiction, and dialogue can be tricky. One thing I've heard about a good novelist is they can envision entire worlds, situations, and all the characters. If you are crafting a fictional realm, you'll need to think of the scenery and settings as vivid and real in your mind. You'll need to convey sensory information about the world; how it feels, what sights and landmarks there are, and consider daytime, nighttime, and the seasons.

You'll also need to know your characters explicitly well. An exercise about character development and understanding is to write a letter from one to another. i.e. if your main character is to interact with another primary character, get into the role like a method actor would and write a personal letter from one to the other.

Be meticulous and think about the emotions of the people and see the perspective of each from a crystal clear point of view. What qualities or traits either disgust or delight the characters on a personal level? Even if you don't share the direct thoughts and ideas from the character letter in your book, it will help you to know your characters better.

You can leave tidbits or secrets sprinkled throughout the story to thread together more profound insights for the reader to discover. Think of Easter Eggs in movies where the audience feels greater inclusion by identifying the obscure allusions.

Authorship is a radically pleasant journey to know. Even if I don't sell millions of copies, there's a definite gratification of crafting something and sharing it with others. Again, I believe every person should write at least one book in their life about anything they want to write.

Don't create words for the sake of words, yet find a person who you want to tell everything, or say something you wish to share to everyone and anyone. The way you form your book is unique to you, though the most vital, crucial, and essential thing is to not focus on the monetary gain;

concentrate on quality and meaning. Many people know this honestly, and the hope is if we write to convey meaning and value, it doesn't matter what we make; just make it. (Is that like the Nike saying of creating?)

I lace signs and symbols into our tapestry. I've used metaphors about seeds, blossoming, and life plus allusions to outer space too. I've also written sections based upon molecular structure, fission and fusion. The twist with metaphors is there are universal symbols we can use. These symbols draw from concepts that others understand mixing in the core of who we are — even saying this is a tapestry calls the ideas of sewing together ideas and thought.

If not to focus on the monetary gain, I'm still tricked up upon this. If I shift from giving free copies to people, it'd mean I need to sell books to get the words to your eyes, and I've been awful with sales. If I create just for people to read, I've also found myself with zero promise or guarantee that another shall read. It's where either passion or obsession drives me to create, regardless of potential readership or gain.

The lessons of self-awareness are substantial, too, from writing. If you choose to edit your work with Grammarly, once the base text forms and you shift to revision, you'll find weird things about your work. When I've worked on my books, I've syphoned signs of cryptic intuition by choosing to write and self-edit.

You also may find bizarre hidden truths about language. Understanding the significance of individual letters found me conscious of words and how they're like Lego blocks of secret guidance. Some of the words I tore to fragments of their constituent parts found me rethinking how I text on my phone.

For example, I became reluctant to use the word 'good' because it had a potential interpretation if split into 'go' and 'od' with no space. It was taken as wishing 'go overdose,' which is not a kind thing. Wishing someone 'good' had a different connotation, and it hounded my neurosis a bit.

I'm kind of ADD with these books. The books' text is

like an Albertan river twisting and turning through the landscape of time, making meanderings and slowly pooling along. We know most rivers lead to a lake or ocean, and if I've repeated time and time again that I want to create for the essential luxury to write what I want, then best I forget the idea of sales and marketing? I've considered both, yet think to myself sometimes I'm creating regardless.

Some of my more 'commercial' projects feel like tasks instead of pleasure. I'm okay to discover more things I love to do to earn $50k+ a year. That's twice as much as I made in 2018, though, and a lot less than setting the goal of selling 15,000 copies a month. I sold less than fifty copies total in the first three years of publishing! I've not entirely detached from the idea of earnings, yet I accept sales to be a bonus and not an expectation.

It may not seem it, yet the remainder is to do what you want to do and release the desire for earnings if they aren't your primary goal. If I were more money-focused, perhaps I'd push for more sales and push for best-seller status. I admit, now, that I'm not entirely comfortable to earn a lower income and not have success with the books.

I've feared how life would be if I had more than I do now. Perhaps my mentality of lack is rooted in a belief of safety because I fear jealousy and greed. If I don't have thousands in my bank account, then no one can steal or mooch it from me, and by not having a car, I don't have to worry about expenses and the responsibility of owning a car. I've not even yet shown I'm responsible enough to earn a basic $30k income by myself, let alone $50k. That changes.

Instead of feeling over-confident or having lingering doubts, I inversely assume success, yet I am nudged to believe in endurance. The pessimistic and optimistic sides polarized again. Perhaps it's best to stop this tangential chapter.

I'm not creating this book for reaching a word count or believing it's going to make me millions. I thought I'd sell books and house multiple people, and if I release pushing for Providing Point, what is the drive that makes me write?

What is my motivation?

I still don't know.

I'm finding my Freedom Solution. I want to be safe, sure, and secure mentally, emotionally, financially, spiritually, socially, and physically. I don't want to be tossed into the cold white-water rapids and fight for survival. I want to be like the slow meandering Albertan rivers carrying the waters of life; where we can sit in the canoe and float along peacefully. The winters in Alberta are ridiculously cold, though, and in spring, summer, and fall, there's also some great life to live there.

So with the theory that all things happen for a reason, I block the text into the book and shift back into my corner. I may not have a coach at this time, yet some people are rooting for me in the audience. I'm reluctant to fight for what I want because I don't want that much. I want to have a life where I can feel the love in my heart for other people without being judgmental of others for how they are living.

We don't all need to have overflowing pockets of cash, yet a bit of coin would be cool. It allows us to build more together in the future.

CORRELATED FAITH

If the most influential and formative years of our lives are when we're kids, that's a sign. I'm an only child, and I don't understand what it's like to be a brother. I was uprooted when I was five from Edmonton to Toronto, and after only three years in Toronto, my family moved to Australia. Two years in Sydney, Australia, and then we moved to Hong Kong for another two or three years. After that, Mom and I came back to Edmonton, which brought me back to being the new kid in school again in grade seven.

It's clear to me now that I've forgotten much of my childhood. I wasn't appropriately socialized, and I'm not in contact with barely anyone from before I was thirteen that isn't family. There are four kids I grew up with until I was five years old; I now call them cousins, though I barely hear from them. They're living their lives, and we rarely speak.

Although it sounds fantastic and glamorous to have lived in Australia and Hong Kong, I recall how I was separate back then. In Australia, I had a best friend named Chris, who tried to teach me how to skateboard and surf, though I wasn't their best friend.

When I lived in Hong Kong, there were many international students, mostly American, though I didn't fit in well there at school. I latched onto another family friend named Ted, and, again, similar to Chris, Ted was my best friend, yet I didn't seem to be his.

I've never really fit in well with groups. In other books, I've talked about playing Survivor, yet how could I excel in a social game? If I've not learned how to buddy up with people and am afraid to speak up sometimes, how could I ever consider having enough game to last past the merge?

Projecting myself isolated and set apart is a particularly unhelpful behaviour. It's not healthy to think of myself of separate; especially if I want to work with others and be part of a tribe. If I attempt to be bold and brave and claim to do some of what I've written in other books, it could make me a target if I am all alone.

The psychiatrists diagnosed me as a paranoid delusional schizophrenic, yet sometimes I wonder how much is having rational fear. The delusions of grandeur from my past have called for some fantastic wishes and wants, yet perhaps I've dreamt, believed, and wished for too much.

As I sat writing this, I thought about where my psychological issues stem from. How many of my problems are from a lack of social graces and understanding and not only mental health issues? My meds null my mind and keep me under control, yet much power holds me within. If there's a chance of me being med-free in my future, I don't know how or when. Some holistic healers believe meds corrupt a mind, and I partly think they may.

When I wrote the first draft of this section, I felt a scummy tingling in my head and shoulders from the medication and felt sketchy tremors thinking about the drugs. Even if I'm not taking recreational drugs, I feel the techy feelings of past psychological damage. Taking medication doesn't make me feel naturally fluid or safe; it seems to feel like chemical corruption. When I've missed one of my meds on rare occasions, the next day feels weird and wonderful, yet later on, the mental activity escalates.

It goes back to the discussion about telepathy. How much of our thoughts are heard or seen by others that aren't us? At the area contest for Toastmasters in March 2019, I was a judge for the speech context. I cognitively heard people reading into my thoughts critically for the scores I was giving. It was not comfortable.

I sometimes think I have zero privacy of my being, and I know when people scrutinize and focus on us, those people can add a great deal of distortion if we're not golden clean. With some of what's ran around in the thoughts I hear sometimes, I agree there are some terrible things and ideas out there.

With awareness being a vital starting point, what happens when we discover our values and ethical acceptability and then build? Some have told me they think I possess strong self-awareness, yet I think I could be called self-absorbed. With my books, I use the word 'I' a lot and don't delve so much into research or reference. If I'm to be market-oriented, then I'll need to know what people want to buy if to be commercially profitable.

Can my self-obsessive lessons, though, be beneficial? Is it best to use me as an example of an overly dramatic and covertly known focal point? When I block the base text of my books, my neurosis seems to stitch waste into the core of the words. Each sentence alone seems not to have value.

Though after reading an entire chapter or volume, and when editing, the words sound more significant. If I am creating a beautiful forest of work, I guess some of the trees aren't so impressive on their own. And yet the seeds find the needs met.

Zeus has been an influential trainer for me. He has tested my boundaries explicitly and is kind and relaxed most of the time. One contested point in our home is him clawing on some pieces of furniture, and it's a behaviour we started to adjust. I'm not clear how ethical my learning is, yet I shall assess and reassess as time progresses.

My behaviours, routines and schedules have been something I'm aware of too. Where in the past I'd fuel up on coffee and work until sunrise, I've more often not, and learnt to respect myself by not abusing so much. Chemical abuse has been an issue with me for a long while, and even if now only the legal drugs of caffeine and nicotine, both addictions have fueled my creative work. They may be part of the cross that I bear.

How could I write a book about being healthy with all of my contaminated choices? I didn't think I could write a book about ethics with some of my unfortunate life choices, though I think we should more often look at our own growth during our lifetimes. Evolution is not only the long-term development of our species or world, but it's also the unstable mutations where we become better and aware of developing acute stability.

I'd love to learn what it's like to be a great parent. Finding the gal to have a child with hasn't yet happened, and there's also a physiological issue I have. I may not be allowed to have kids. Medicine has developed a long way, so perhaps DNA splicing ensues, yet adoption isn't off the table from my view. I prefer that my child be my flesh and blood, though if that's not physically possible, I'll need to talk about it with my wife.

Honestly, though, I'm not sure why I want to be a parent. I'm not sure if it's so that my parents can have grandkids, though I think it's because it would be awesome to socialize and raise another fantastic human; especially with a woman I love and respect.

Thinking about having a kid and *having* a child is entirely different, yet it's a dialogue I want to have. I believe being a parent would be a rewarding journey to share with a gal, and it stems from me wishing I had my own family.

Watch what you wish for, though, right? I've wished to meet Natalie, and I've wanted to live in the Glass House. I also hoped Providing Point be a charity to home 250,000 people as an organization. I feel nowhere near reaching any of those three goals.

What have you wanted that you have near zero belief it shall manifest? Maybe if we work more for our wishes, we can help them come into being.

And then the light courses down from galactic realms into the soul. As we carry forward with the text, subtle unions of thought nudge the cursor across the page, yet when you see the words, the book shall be complete.

When we read books, we don't understand all that's gone into forming them; from the initial idea or impulse, the editing and revision, and the subtle thoughts, hesitations, and inspirations that press each key. It's a miraculous process.

I bring this back to other writers. I may not have tons of recommendations or much guidance for you, and if you are a seasoned writer, then I may look daft and amateur. Endurance and continuation of forming books hold a value, though it may not always be transactional in a clear and concise form. Sly adaptations of text hint and the developments of the glaciers developing.

And yet the warm water and light course from above to rinse off my spirit. Even if you see the same words, there's variety in how others hear it. If another hears us speak and we're telling the truth, it may not be factual for them.

Inversely true, if another is honestly a kind, decent, and honourable person, it still may seem they are goading and at fault. Another different person could be spiteful, filled with malice and disdain, yet always be believed to love. Some speak gentle and kind, yet a torrent of energy hurls their mind against walls of belief. And, yet again, another may seem angry and hateful, yet just be out of sorts and misunderstood as a person.

The balance and shift of good and evil can polarize understanding. I have been afraid of calling myself good because of the saying, "only the good die young." Though the lyric haunted me many years ago in my youth, another reminded me I'm not so young anymore.

It brings us to Saturn and the bringer of old age. I may have misconceived the association though found the link from the album *Holst: The Planets*. I had an idea to call this three-part book *Saturn's Rings*. It was after the first draft was done that I thought of the title *Mosaic of Miracles*.

If I keep cycling ideas about dreams and notions of my being, is that a metaphor of how I'm like a noble gas? It seems I don't bond with many very well, and I feel further away from the Sun than most Earthlings. In some mythology and symbolism, Christ is said to be the Sun; the star we orbit.

Part of my life is still tethered to Him, though I've fallen far away from worshiping. I pray, though not near as often as I used to. I'm concerned about sacrificing myself entirely and wish to gain courage. What compounds is my human fear of giving myself away to anyone or anything? It's because I'm afraid I'll lose myself. I seem to teeter in between my beliefs. It's not so much like a pendulum swinging between two points for a pendulum appears more secure. I sometimes feel like I'm walking a tightrope wobbling and wavering without having a stable balance.

Though some say when we're wavering between points without certainty that that's the sweet spot of living. When we are on the precipice or cusp of an unknown experience or truth, we can feel quite alive. It's the uncertainty and nervousness that can turn into fear or excitement; it depends on how we respond to the insecurities. Language may seem very explicit, and when reading a book, we see the long game of an idea.

My weaves may be sporadic, yet the process of extending the series straightens out some things. There are frayed threads, yet the needle points of one chapter after the next stitch together something I hope may warm a few hearts. I'm fortunate to have a home and place to sleep, and part of me believes if I keep at sheltering ideas on the pages of these books, we'll flourish. It may be another couple of years until we see the results, and sadly, I lack the faith we provide.

When I typed this, I realized I might lack some desirable things, mainly money, though I have a massive abundance of other things. Even when broke, I still feel rich in some ways. Without being popular or hearing from friends, it's a luxury to have such an amount of time, space, and freedom from the demands of others. Famous people have all sorts of random people messaging and reaching out to them all the time. I don't have that, and I appreciate the lack of attention.

I lack influence too, though, which could be helpful to generate and do some things. If I had a more significant impact on life, what would I do? At this moment, I realize I'm in a vacuum of attention. I can gain clarity and focus on choosing what I'll do. In line with The Fountains of Fantasy, perhaps I can write about what we can do with massive influence or money.

I've thought I've been poor money wise for a few reasons. I've been concerned about mooches and thieves, and I've thought if I have cash, that another would want it from me. I've even thought about responsibility and how I've been foolish with money in the past. Wondrously, I increase my resources, yet substantial acquisition and book sales could not be okay if I'm not responsible.

Regarding what I would or will do if I reach a high level of prosperity? I also need to think about what can I do to achieve a high level of well-being. If I can sell thousands of books, I know that the 51% from the three-part books and 100% from the individual Fountain books go to where I promised in Fountain six, though what of the 49%?

If I sell three thousand books a month, it'll mean I'll be earning about $7,000 a month from books. Making that much can easily cover my debts, allow me a vehicle, and put me towards and into a new home. The question then, how do I sell three thousand books a month?

In the second and third month of 2019, I'd started telling people my goal of selling a hundred units of me a day. That's more than the fifty I wrote about in the second chapter, though I still believe if we set higher goals, we have more to work for. It shall be a process and require effort, luck, and support, yet I'm starting to believe in it. *"How do you eat an elephant? One bite at a time."*

If that holds as truth, then I must start grain by grain, bit by bit, seed by seed, and book by the book. I understand it's a pathway I walk, though fortunately some walk alongside. My friends, family, and contacts would appreciate it if I'm not going to sell them a book or solicit a pledge, yet I'll be able to share more as I reach my sales goals. Considering the potential, I'm hoping it shall be profitable.

I best be cautious, though. If I can reach selling three thousand units per month, there may be more focus on me and what I do. With my nervousness and excitement of thinking about reaching so many people, I'll also need to accept more may be asked of me. That's part of the responsibility; if I am to reach a vast audience, I owe homage, respect, and regard to you and them too. It's my readers that also allow me to live the life I lead.

GIVE IN OR GIVE UP?

I needed to reinvent and rediscover a new set of wants and desires. What I had been doing wasn't working, and the day I first wrote this, I became very vulgar, angry, and abusive.

After writing a bit, I called my Mom, and it was an excellent choice. I remember Mom's advice from when I was growing up about 'needing an attitude adjustment.' It's very accurate and happened again a few weeks later.

Fountains ten to twelve are the Fountains of Fantasy. In them, I want to write more of what I want to happen, yet needed to repent. I shifted to optimism after feeling mad and angry with my life, and know who I am doesn't always coincide with how I behave. I wish for love, hope, happiness, and truth, though the fact when I wrote this was I honestly wasn't that thrilled.

Depression is a legitimate thing, yet there also can be bullish and persistent defiance. I've had considerable uncertainty about what I want, why I want it, and how I want to feel, and the day I first wrote this chapter is NOT how I want to be. I needed to get out of the space and mindset I was within; I needed to breathe, centre, reset and make a new take. Gratitude is helpful, and it is tricky to get off a negative train of thought.

Whining and complaining is a waste of time, effort, and energy. I need to focus on the present, think of what I want for the future, and also remember that the past is a substantial portion of our life here on Earth. Some may not forgive, some people may wish they knew love, and sometimes I need to remember that it's a small number of people that genuinely do care for me.

If I want love in my life, I'm going to have to go out there and earn it. At home, living with my cat was awful for a while. I was getting angry and abusive because of Zeus intentionally clawing on furniture. Zeus knows it makes me mad when he scratches, and it seems to be a blatant power play.

Some say cats don't understand English, though I hold firm a belief they also must know what anger is. They're not stupid; they are smart and crafty animals that know full well how to assert power and demand control. That's what happened the first weeks Zeus lived with me, and the power struggle surfaced again.

Instead of focusing and expressing how I'd been feeling anger, resentment, and hatred, I want to use this chapter to build, not destroy. It's going to be tough to create a life of peace, love, unity, and respect with how I've been acting, though the shift is towards earning, developing, and cultivating love and not just money.

Peace with ourselves is the first thing we need. For me to find inner peace, I need to acknowledge and accept myself. It's a tough one because often I don't like myself. I've been triggered easily and angered, and when I get angry, vulgarities hurl out of my mouth, and I want to smash things. I've done so too sometimes.

When violent, I've ruined non-animate objects and have wanted to decimate some living too. I don't like that part about myself. I want love, though why would anyone want to love me? If I know my actions aren't admirable and I've lashed out, then how could I ever earn love?

I see being peaceful as a precursor to love, and I have understood how someone can be violent and also be loving. Abusive relationships see that, and repentant or remorseful feelings are legitimate. It's a very bizarre dualism though I understand it from myself; a part I'm not proud of.

If trapped in repentant energy, it's difficult to free from such. The same thing goes for self-hate or even the emotion of grief. When we aren't feeling good about ourselves or others, we need to find ways to climb out of the pits of despair.

I'm learning how to do so and have a firm belief that talk

therapy is fantastic. When we can openly and honestly state our grievances, or acknowledge our mistakes to those we've wronged or resent, it can be a path towards peace.

If you argue and win an argument, though, you also may win hate, spite, and anger. Is it worth it? I don't think it is. The title *Give In or Give Up* stemmed from me either giving in and being dominated, or give up and release any care, compassion or kindness for Zeus. I didn't see that it a win/win in either way; it couldn't even seem to be a compromise.

Giving up could have been avoiding conflict, and submitting and accepting terrible behaviour would have been giving in. Both could build resentments and result in an unfortunate situation.

My life to many is irrelevant and not even trivial, and if I yearn to procure the values of inclusion, compassion, and kindness from myself and others, I must adjust when I turn into my angry and vulgar version of self; I must remember to return to and honour my peaceful and loving side.

I do feel guilt and shame, though I need to process them and not contaminate another. It's a reason I keep myself away from some others sometimes; so I don't taint the waters of life when I get poisonous.

If I want to push away every moment of life, where can I be if the cat lives with me? He was disrespectful, and I felt aggravated and goaded. I felt like I wanted to throw him off the balcony. So if I didn't like his behaviour, give up?

If I gave up, it would have released any kindness and forgiveness I have for him. It may sound magnified, yet his spiteful and vindictive actions aroused me to hate. I was living with an infestation of negativity and degradation, and I found myself wanting to hurt the cat and damage him.

I won't inflict physical damage upon Zeus, yet I had locked him up in his kennel when he clawed on the furniture. That didn't dissuade him either. I'd love to hear from Zeus about his grievances, yet that isn't an option either because he doesn't speak English. The spiralling thoughts and feelings wished retribution, yet that isn't positive either.

If hate begets hate, and we're fueled by the ones we live with, we can't always just kick them out of our home. The experience with Zeus was entrapment, yet I know he can't just leave either. I knew we'd find a solution, even if we didn't know what it was.

Persistence, patience, and consequence created me being passive and accepting, yet, with some, I refuse to share the same space. Retaliation isn't a kind thing, and there is an argument about the consequences of actions. How can we be peaceful if we're goaded by another who wants us to be angry?

The situation with Zeus got me thinking about prisons and corrections institutions. Putting anyone in confinement can only further bury and burrow spite and hatred. With humans and prisons, the theory is that we can minimize poor behaviour with the threat of locking someone up in a cell. If someone is put through such, though, I can see how their psyche and self-worth might believe they aren't or can't be decent people again.

With my cat, I saw that if I lock him up, he may spitefully claw on the furniture again from disliking being punished. It seemed like a negative cycle, yet I keep my responsibility by not harming him. That's where the control needed is self-control and not animal control.

When I typed this, I didn't see or believe punishments of kennel time or being locked up in a room were beneficial or a solution. How can we believe in the goodness of another if they're violent, abusive, or vulgar? I understand the negative cycle, and if anyone is treated like they're only going to do wrong, how can we even expect them to be good, kind, and peaceful?

My expectations were way off. Even if I want to be loving, sweet, kind, and gracious, bad behaviours have triggered me to reciprocate hate and separate. Since I don't want to return hatred or animosity, I put Zeus in a different room, and in other situations, have removed myself from where I've been.

With human friends, I've also separated from some connections. I have been easily triggered, and when I catch myself turning venomous, I practice learning how to respond and how to be appropriate. I dislike violence and abuse, yet during the two weeks with Zeus, they seemed like highly logical reactions.

If anything was gained from difficult times, it's both a comprehension of feelings I'm not used to and learning how to behave, control, and minimize them. When broken, mutual respect and love can return, though it takes time. I couldn't expect to control or manage my cat's behaviour, and I certainly couldn't discuss it with him.

It was exceptionally petty and pitiful how I got so reactive; I understand there are issues I need to deal with. I wondered how the resolution would manifest and thought positive reciprocation was a fantasy. Working together with mutual respect was and is the solution, yet I can't command that from another, especially a cat.

So, what's happened since those few tricky weeks? I've again wanted to travel to Italy, and I've wanted to own a car. I've been working part-time as a landscaper, cleared my student loans, and also have been progressing with the books.

I love Zeus now, even if I disliked his previous behaviours. To solve the issue with clawing, he has a cat tree and a scratching post (which, yes, the scratching post was there during the trials and tribulations), and three carefully placed towels were put on the contested spots.

It's a fact I've not had much love in my life, yet I desire human interaction and wish to have more. I sorted out my attitude adjustment, and I'm not sure how to find a girlfriend and build our life together. That's one of the next steps.

In March 2019, I hated myself and my life. I'm not entirely clear on what happens in the future, yet I'm glad I didn't give up on Zeus and deny him a home. Is that what the world would have done with me?

Theoretically, the world dislikes my behaviour also, so it

seems some have given up on me and leave me alone without contact. I don't want my home to be a prison cell for Zeus and me, so perhaps I can view it instead as a safe haven and place of solitude where we are abundant in time, space, and connection.

I'd not felt as much anger towards someone in the two years before that March. I've bitched and moaned about work, yet having a job, a home, a cat, and resources are actually fantastic blessings. Being locked up without having space for oneself is different than being alone.

If I like having my own space, then I also think of parenting human children. Kids are a lifelong commitment, and not a commitment many can back out of most of the time. Some kids are given up for adoption, and abortion is a thing, though I commend the parents that tough it out with their offspring.

What though can one do about another animal living in their home? What can be done when a situation comes near to or is violent? I've seen parts of the dark side of life, and it's an unsettling understanding. What I'd like to know is the solution to evil thoughts and feelings to prevent them in others too.

It also got me thinking about marriage and divorce. How bad can it be that there is a divorce? As much as I didn't like it, I comprehend how hate and animosity can become too much. With Zeus, I saw a side of human emotion I'd never fully known, and I'm glad I forget it.

With Zeus, in some ways, I believe he knows what's right and wrong. If he does what he wants anyhow, perhaps I can give him more good things to do. The lesson was; when others abuse us by triggering our tender points, we can turn into monsters.

I don't want to carry negativity in my being. If it's helpful to get out of a toxic relationship, it may be beneficial for both. Unfortunate situations can turn out okay, though. That's happened for Zeus and me too. I thought living with a cat would be love, kindness, and affection, though it wasn't that way for part of our process.

March 2019's trauma was a call for love and respect, and it's due to a cat who refused to give in. Living with another isn't easy, and it was profoundly proven to me. I questioned my mental health and understand how abusive, demeaning, and reactive I can be. I wish not to be that way.

Here's a weird thought for the world:

If there is a God, then He created science. If God created science and doesn't want to be known, then science cannot prove He exists. If God wants to be understood, yet not by anyone who believes only in science, then science will never be able to prove He exists. If someone believes entirely in God and uses science to determine His existence, if God doesn't want anyone to prove His existence with science, even a believing scientist cannot prove God exists. If God wants people to genuinely believe in Him in their own understanding or way, then He will be faithful to them in the ways only that person may know; thus not being recognized in the same way by anyone.

I can't prove I love, and I've also shown I'm capable of hate. It may be very few that are or believe I'm a friend, yet I seem to sense those who present as friends don't like me so much. I've thought some are part of the plot, and though I don't like how I was with Zeus in our rough spot, the past few weeks remind me my authentic nature is love.

Perhaps this chapter is sufficiently titled. I wouldn't give in and submit, so maybe I gave up and release. Another part of this is my compassionate side believed and thought there could be a situation where Zeus and I wouldn't struggle for power. With his attempt of dominant behaviour, I was sure I needed to clear the cat from home, and with such a substantial adverse effect on my demeanour, I found me hating myself and others when I was around them. I didn't want to be in that type of relationship with myself or another.

The blend of self-care tangled with submissive compassion and thorough animosity. If I submitted and let Zeus scratch on the furniture without repercussions, I'd only resent him more. Another pathway would be to release any attachments to my quality of life and attitude and let him rule the home. No. I didn't want that either.

I almost gave him up. Sorry, Zeus. Though you pushed me far too far and I wanted to obliterate you, it seemed you intended to aggravate me and push me to my limits. From a few pages ago: "If you win an argument, you also may win hate, spite, and anger." That is what you won for a while, Zeus, though I didn't give in or give up. We found a different pathway.

MEDIATED MOTIVATION

I fuel reality into fantasy. The previous chapter was stemmed from the power struggle I had with my cat, and though that point of time included some of the darker and harsh elements of myself, it taught me a bit about abusive relationships. I believe in healing, repentance, and reparations, though if this is the first of the three Fountains of Fantasy, let's get back to dreaming.

I've been open at times about helping others with money and resources because I want to help people other than myself. I've held dreams of my own successes, yet for the three to four weeks before this chapter, I was working landscaping, my classes had just finished for the semester, and I'd gotten money-focused again.

With earning from my job and liking such, I repent I've also received a lot for free. If to make money, what to do with it? Some want to buy expensive things or high-value items, while I'd like to pay off my debts. I owe money to the government and also to the bank, and though I had student loans, I paid them off in July 2019. I also want to own my home outright and save for the future. That requires earnings and planning.

One item I would like to buy is a car. I've gone without a car for three years, though the lure of putting money towards my debts is strong. Instead of buying a car, I'd like to keep money free for other things, and once my debts are paid, I can look at building a home and gathering a down payment for it.

If I build and live in the home I see in my mind, the Glass House, it's going to require significant earnings. Working landscaping isn't anywhere near enough to provide for the home, yet I can envision each room of the house. It seems like book royalties are probably not the pathway to the home yet either, but they hold a substantial role in its construction.

By seeing and hearing how my boss is with his company, it's evident running a business is *not* an easy thing. In 2018, I thought I was going to run Providing Point as an open and expansive organization, yet charitable work isn't going to earn me an income. Another business could be potentially profitable, though, the concept of gathering for an NGO remind me the money is for others and not me.

In earlier books, I promised book earnings to go to charities, and I maintain those promises. I also wonder if I'd have more success with books, sales, and marketing if I profited more from the process of authorship. I need to sell myself on the point of the books being great reads and that the program is worthwhile and valuable.

In a movie, I heard one thing about being an adult is to fail miserably at something we love. At this point, it seems I have been unable to achieve my dreams. I've not yet met Natalie, I've not again turned Providing Point into a thriving non-profit, and I've written almost a dozen books without profiting substantially.

I've not quit, though. Even if I've not yet earned much from my books, writing, for me, is something I feel impelled to do. The dreams are still there; sell lots of books, gather interest and pledges, be debt-free, and move forward.

Some pledges may come from talking about the program with the confidence needed to find people who want to ally. I realize, as much as I'd like otherwise, it truly matters what I do and say. I fell from being high in the clouds and then landed pleasantly on stable ground.

It's kind of comforting, though, to know I don't have to tend to thousands of fans. I live a peaceful and sometimes dull life, yet my cat Zeus is here. Even if it's not always been true, Zeus is a perfect point of love, and I feel a bit of sadness and shame for my abusive actions of the past. My cat is very dear to me, my heart, and my soul, and I hope to gain his forgiveness and his love.

My Dad and step-dad have read some of my books, and these books are how I send out my wishes to the universe. In an open exposition, the hope is we can continue to sort out and refine aspirations, goals, and dreams. Sands shift along the shorelines of time, yet I remember to amend and add a tad of PLU8R with the rhyme. Repentance is a genuine thing.

April 18th, 2019

Okay, I can explicitly choose to write anything I want to. With the intent to see the book in its final form, we remember the cast's view of how she doesn't know you too.

My girlfriend hadn't yet visited my apartment, yet she might have been thinking about this for a while. I remind Zeus that Mooshka and Belle also weirdly believe in love. I hope I can write for the sake of writing and allow the right things to happen for us. God, please enable us to thrive.

I wasn't clear I could write to Aeris again. Aeris is my future daughter. I wrote to her in the 4th Fountain, and upon revision, I wondered about that text because, as far as I can yet hope or imagine, it's just Zeus and me here.

Hopefully, two kittens (Mooshka and Belle) can move in after I hook up with my real lovestone, and it seems logical to find real love instead of Natalie; especially since the enchantment may be removed.

A question to ask when writing. Who are we writing to? An active part evolves what we're saying, though if I write to one person, even if myself, a focused chain of text ensues. If written to a broad audience, perhaps generalization could dilute, so to whom I best direct the words?

I didn't have a girlfriend when I first typed this, and if to write to another, I could mix up parameters. What about a letter to God? Or, I could generally write out to the Universe again. If my next girlfriend reads this book (or the others), she'll have a window into my being, yet since I don't reveal so much verbally, if she reads the books, she'll know a lot.

You'll see and understand how I've been galactically outlandish, and even if so foolishly optimistic, I've achieved abysmal results from my bookwork up to now. I prefer to talk instead of text, and sometimes a phone call is as good as an in-person meeting, yet my dear love, where are you?

Sometimes I don't want to meet up with people, and in those cases, sometimes a phone call is entirely okay. There are a rare few I'd love to talk with and can't for they don't answer the phone or return messages. It's also rare that people are up late when I write during the night. I could better heed hints and learn to be more respectful and considerate.

Who are you, though? Living alone, even with Zeus here, it's an ultra-basic life with so few people to talk to. I have about four hundred contacts on my phone, yet there's only a narrow few I can call out to if I want to talk. Of lots of the others, I either don't want to bother them, don't feel safe to contact them, or want to avoid reaching out to them.

Of the twenty or so people on my favourites list, less than one third can I call if I just want to talk. It's also tricky to call someone when it's near 3 AM in the morning. When I wake up, I don't have a human to talk with as the first thing of my day, yet in my ideal situation, I'd have a person to chat with and plan the day (and more distant future) with in the morning.

Zeus and I's relationship has improved a lot in the past few weeks. Though I can't talk with Zeus, I can learn to be more intuitive. Some people say we limit ourselves by saying, 'I can't,' but some things are technically not an option. I wrote about how we can't make people care, yet we can till the seeds.

Brad, my boss, gave me the next day off. I deep-cleaned my bathroom and noticed how I'm starting to care more about my home and the quality of life there. It's a radically good thing to have a job, yet I'd like to have more time at home to work on the computer too.

I wonder about my music and what I can do with it.

Similar to my books, I've created a bunch, yet I've not generated or earned much money with my recordings either. I posted a track called Matrix on SoundCloud the night I wrote this to share with a friend named Glenna.

I referred to Glenna as a kind glass of champagne before, yet I believe I shouldn't sip from her glass. She's radically kind and refreshing and has always been talkative with me, yet she's still quite young. That's been an issue with a few gals I like and appreciate, yet I also should check and keep my intents. In a chapter I wrote to Elspeth, I wrote and remind us, "I shouldn't be doing things like a twenty-year-old."

Have you heard of the 'half the age plus seven rule'? If you're older, divide your age by two and then add seven; that's the boundary of age allowance. I'm 41, so 28 is my boundary. Dating someone older than 28 and younger than 45 is my preference, and if we live for a few decades, I hope I don't have to grieve my love as a loss. Is that a reason why I'd prefer a younger gal?

From 2018, it's clear I don't want to feel grief. It may be a reason I keep from loving some friends and family too much also; I know how terrible loss can feel. I don't want to lose people, and even if they say it's better to have loved and lost, then never have loved at all, I feel uneasy.

Check-in with yourself right now. Who are the people you know that are explicitly clear as ones who you can trust and also love you in return? Some are trustworthy, though distant, and some may like us, yet we can't confirm the truth.

My paranoid side tips me into how some friends are authentically safe and honest, while others could be conspirators. I rarely feel entirely confident about who is trustworthy. I also desire to share my illogical pathways of thought in text with you. I want to share what I've thought and why, though if no one reads what I've written, there's still a cognitive element. People hear what I type and think when forming these books.

Zeus is a thought conduit, and I've sometimes thought

what I vocalize or feel at home is amplified by him. When communicating ideas to others, that's where a belief in ESP, telepathy, or group think mixes in with linguistics. If multiple languages are woven into threads of speech, text, or thought, potentially diverse networks and nodes of people hear and understand. Strings of communication in different languages piece together fragments of our mind, body, spirit, and soul by stitching together parts of the tapestry of life.

The various representations of symbolism also are only shards of a coherent whole, and yet we're consciously and contialitically aligned via the choices, connections, and functions that resume. I don't hold dominion over anything on this planet, and yet with grace, forgiveness, and compassion, I hope well to endure.

I've had concerns about plots and plans while at home and out and about, yet I mustn't let fear dissuade me from thriving. The nighttime is a place I love, and though not at 'er as much as I used to be, it's a place within which to create.

A bit of Christy Whitman's advice; three questions. What do I want? Why do I want it? How do I want to feel? The writing recommendation from me; three questions to answer. Who are you telling? What are you telling them? Why should they know? And, from neurosis; three questions to consider. Who's causing the nervousness? Do I need to pause and reset? What may I do to use this energy productively?

Psychosis is synergistically complex, and it's like a cryptic message obfuscated by the truth. Sometimes it's plainly apparent who we best not trust or contact, and our hearts seem to compound with faith. The wish and hope are we can have friends that want to support us and also want us to be there to meld.

Why should I write these books? If people read them, what do people gain from them? If I put truth into text, how and why could that benefit the world? If my thoughts are all filibuster or nonsense, how is this helping another? What gains are received from putting these words one after the next?

The sequence matters, yet spelling scatters the debris of language across landscapes of time. My kitten reminds me how to love and be kind, yet I filter doubt about me being lovable. I've detested myself and my actions when I get angry and reactive, and I've felt shameful and repentant for misgivings and transgressions I've made.

Hesitantly, I move the cursor across the page while conspirators loom in my psyche. I yearn for genuine care, hope, and devotion and am committed to the process as I set myself aside. I wish for peace and love too.

I don't know who I'm telling right now. I'd like to know. Reverently and abashedly, I think of how it was Easter weekend the Thursday night I wrote this. Delusions, hallucinations, and fantastically whistful notions of the past called with a thirst for our future.

We cannot save humanity with wishes and wants, and I don't think faith can lure my lucrative lunacy. Lustful liaisons call codal collisions of constellations, yet callously contested correction calms creativity. It may be best for the next few months to assist in securing some hope and faith.

I may not earn the big money and big prizes from writing, yet gains are made into the future. Sanity is a precious thing, and parts of these books help me hone in on what is right and just. People could be upset that I'm up late again tonight (it was 1:37 AM), yet fortunately, I was getting a bit tired, and this chapter was almost complete. I thank You for allowing me to write this, and hope much more is allowed to form.

Molto Grazie, Dio... Amen.

FUZZY LOGIC

The night I wrote the first bits of this section, I thought of the 10th Fountain book's earnings. The idea of who to give the profits get twisted up and in. There are organizations I'd like to assist with funding, though considering sales up to now, I'm not clear that much shall come from the individual Fountain books. It's highly probable the three-part books shall be more significant earners than the individual books, though I can't guarantee that either.

One thought from before I finished the second Fountain was to have multiple books for sale to increase earnings. I know it's a manipulation tactic, though the idea is if people want to own *all* the books, they can buy separate copies like collectables. I didn't know back then I'd give 100% of the earnings from individual Fountains to different causes, and I also didn't plan to receive 49% of the three-part Fountains books.

A twist of my selfishness surfaces with Providing Point. I'd like to earn more personal money, and from a conversation with a planeswalker friend, I wondered what happens if Providing Point does expand. An idea is to make a salary from the program. In the irrational dream world, if Providing Point does develop and grow, we might need additional employees, yet as of 2019, I was the only employee operating the program. I thought we could find another win/win.

I asked the then-current providers about receiving a small percentage of the Patreon earnings. This seems a bit sly, yet could earning some money motivate me to work and gather more? If we reach a high level of gathering, 1% of the earnings could be quite profitable. The lure of the gain would shift to profit motivation, not intrinsically about providing.

When I asked one of the providers about garnering 1%

of the earnings, they suggested 5%. 5% isn't much right now, yet honestly, it could be lucrative. As of October 2019, we had US$136 a month gathered from eight providers. 1% would mean $1.36, and 5% is $6.80 a month. That's not even an hour of a minimum wage.

Gathering income from a charitable cause isn't entirely ethical in my view, and if to thrive and register as an NGO, a portion would be needed for operating expenses; legal fees, incorporation, an accountant, and future employees. If we reach the point of Full Seed, complete coverage, the percentages could be substantial.

I've written that the value of one Yearly Seed as $15,128. If we provide 600 Yearly Seeds, that means 1% is $90,768 per year. If increased to 5%, that would mean $453,840 per year for 600 Seeds. That's a significant amount and could provide for additional employees.

A personal goal on my vision board is to provide 1,000 people homes from my book earnings. How can that happen? If we work Introversial as a for-purpose, for-profit, Providing Point's power to provide could be significant. As of October 2019, Providing Point and Introversial were not registered companies, and Providing Point had $346.59 in account; enough to cover the next three months of $15/month Share and Care cards.

I'm aware I sometimes like to give money and things, yet I also love to receive and earn. Even if individual Fountains' earnings go entirely to charities or causes, I still feel more invested in the three-part books. The three-parters earn me money, yet I've been focused on the split of working for no personal gain and squirrelling a living for myself too.

Because of potential earnings from Fountains books and a belief I'm finally starting to release good books, I have more confidence in books like *Shards of My Soul* to sell. Even if *Rings of Truth* sells well, it'll be a while until *Mosaic of Miracles*, the next three-part book, is available for sale. I also need to decide what to do with the book *Shared Node*.

Shared Node is a book of rhymes, yet I've not allocated

earnings. Perhaps more recordings manifest from the book, and after being a rhymer for twenty years, I shouldn't neglect my music. My first recording was in 1999, and though my musical productions are amateur, I've increased my mental agility and skill. I've learned more about my rhymes and flow, and even if not Hip-Hop or Rap, the music is pretty cool.

The albums Shandalite, Digital Slipstate, Matricite, and Signal to Node are available on Spotify, iTunes, Google Play, YouTube, and Amazon, yet if you want to find more of my music, go to www.KoyichDigital.Bandcamp.com. There are about ten or so albums available for streaming or download there. 51% of the earnings go to Providing Point, and if I focus on music distribution, and I'd like to know if posting tracks is a good idea.

The idea of one or five percent fluxes into my mind again. This program is too much about me and what I make or gain instead of running a non-profit. Readership and listeners can purchase the music and books without a monthly pledge, and if the purpose of the Patreon site is to gather and provide for those who need and want help, then I should be the guide, not the focal point.

If other creators pledge their work to Introversial's page, could they receive rewards too? I must find ways to improve, bolster, and add to the program and process to increase efficiency, and if there is a potential for gathering more pledges, I realize I still feel hesitant.

I'm concerned about massive expansion and wonder how to pursue the program. I'm not sure it's the right thing, for the right reasons, though if it is, and if we can assure it's for the right people, perhaps the idea is a valuable and one that many shall aid and tend.

If we operate Providing Point as a company, when we reach the point of twenty cardholders, then perhaps I can rethink the wage portion. Until then, I work as a volunteer for Providing Point's Introversial branch.

Boundaries and expectations must be clear, concise, and

openly shown and known. Neither Introversial or Providing Point were yet registered companies, though managing the cards and accounts require ethical behaviour. It may be too soon to speak with all the people involved, yet conversations with the cardholders and providers through the next few months are valuable. We're an open and honest company working for our community with gradual expansion.

Some people say to do what's best for ourselves, and a Utilitarian viewpoint would be to do what's best for everyone. If working for personal gain can benefit many others, generating pledges and sales is a good idea. I want to provide, and I want to earn. If I can't make enough on my own to share a lot, then perhaps I can encourage others to help those who the program is meant for.

I waffled on percentages with the book earnings for a couple months, and in the two or three weeks before the base of this chapter, my opinions, guilt, and hope bundled a muddled intent. With three friends, they thought I should allocate 10% of the Patreon earnings for administration on the premise Introversial may need additional employees. I'm not clear we shall, though if we do, it's a few years from now.

It's cleaner in my heart and soul for me to not earn from the Providing Point Patreon gathering. It could be a win/win lure for me to work and promote, though I believe if I receive earnings, it might dilute the company. I've thought of running the company as an extension of myself and my creative work for profit, yet it's a community idea and program, not for me to make money.

I shared 65 copies of the 8th Fountain with no additional pledges given from sharing the book. Because the book talks about Providing Point and its premises, I believed sharing the 8th Fountain would gather patrons and more interest in the program. We didn't see that result. I think I need more motivation to collect pledges.

At some points, I've wanted to work solely as an author and sell, while other times, I've wanted to gather and share money and grocery cards. Money can assist and help, yet it's not the only variable. Money can help provide homes for people, and that can change the outlook of some who think they're living in Hell.

It was early August 2019 at this point. We had four $15/month cards in distribution, and I felt good about the people who held cards. I've not known many suitable for the program, and because of my paranoid delusional sides of self, I'd not been confident on street level. Many need support, and I'd been working alone a lot. We had eight pledges, yet I couldn't imagine a hundred or more at that juncture.

I am skeptical of street-level activity. I have fears about connecting with random street people to find more cardholders, yet I received a recommendation to contact Ruth and Naomi's. Anne Davis also can find more good seeds; people who need additional support and are kind and decent. Who are the right people to gain support, though?

Mixed up into all of this is the question: "Does it even matter?" How do these years of bookwork and a passive activist viewpoint affect the big picture? If I was gone, how would Providing Point operate? If the program was thriving, would it be more appreciated? I've sometimes thought the conspiracies are aimed at me for making proclamations, yet I wonder too, how many people know about me and my ideas? Does it matter if I write? I hope it does.

I like to write, yet my texts are so much about me and my wishful ideas. I've written a bit about my neurotic fears and obsessions, and I've also discussed often my lack of hope, faith, and confidence. Writing is a valuable thing to do, yet how can my work be useful for other people too? I've thought the dissemination of ideas can be beneficial, yet how would the world be if we activated them? Perhaps that's a section title to rewrite; *What if it all Happened?*

Rationally, I think I don't care enough for myself and my dreams. I've found I care well for others in heart, yet not in action. Other times, my obsessions suffocate, and my fear of lack and lack of faith inspire me to communicate. Writing may be too passive an activity and not efficient enough to gather resources for community support.

Money has been a lure and motivation for me often, yet I also think a profit-driven focus can impel me productively. Conversely, generosity, giving, and sharing are things I like and love to do. We need to have something before we can share it; that applies to knowledge too.

Perhaps I need to get back to learning, studying and reading new material. The book *Zero to One* by Peter Thiel was what sparked part of the Providing Point resurgence, and I have two other books that might help with seeding motivation for the cause; The *1-Page Marketing Plan* by Allan Dib and *Building a Story Brand* by Donald Miller.

A couple weeks slipped in between sections. I received another book in the mail to read; *How to Write Copy that Sells* by Ray Edwards. The mix of the business books gets me psyched up and inspired about Providing Point, yet my activities also impel me to work for personal gain. In the week before, I had a coaching call with a QSCA coach that suggested I write a wishlist for a girlfriend. I thought I may have had a chance with Elspeth, though she seems to have chosen another.

Impatience, my Dad would tell me, can lure delusions. Fretful and jittery, the caffeine reminds me I'm afraid to sleep. Why cannot a nice rest seep kindly and comfortably into my desires? Why must money be the motivation, when the desire is a relationship? Another belief cues me to think that if the connection is the desire, then I best share abundantly with those I connect with.

Prerogatives of thought beckon for resolve, yet resolve isn't, however, an R of PLU8R. What shall be the resolution?

Why are my vagrant whims of heart calling for fortitude? Why do my fantasies seem to lead to wandering backwards from where I want to be? With pressure in my cranium, it's like I'm pushing and fighting to have meaning while evading purposes others wish me to have.

I have dreams, yet seem to relish in being alone where I'm allowed to write and work. How can I claim to be love, when all I am is myself? Why don't I wake up in the mornings happy to be alive?

It's like a locomotive; my days and my life. It takes a long while to get going, and then it seems like I cannot or don't want to stop.

One nighttime dream I saw had a train engine blast into a cement wall. The impact tremor visually resonated with a wave of sound and energy that looked like deep water ripples.

I hope I don't need to crash, and it's clear I am pushing against the walls. Perhaps I need to switch tracks and carry more of my being to a peaceful and romantic destination.

ROBERT KOYICH

ROBERT KOYICH

ROBERT KOYICH

ROBERT KOYICH

ROBERT KOYICH

ROBERT KOYICH

ROBERT KOYICH

ROBERT KOYICH

ROBERT KOYICH

ROBERT KOYICH

ROBERT KOYICH

ROBERT KOYICH

ROBERT KOYICH

ROBERT KOYICH

ROBERT KOYICH

ROBERT KOYICH

ROBERT KOYICH

ROBERT KOYICH

ROBERT KOYICH

ROBERT KOYICH

ROBERT KOYICH

ROBERT KOYICH

ROBERT KOYICH

ROBERT KOYICH

ROBERT KOYICH

ROBERT KOYICH

ROBERT KOYICH

ROBERT KOYICH

ROBERT KOYICH

Stop.

ROBERT KOYICH

ROBERT KOYICH

GET THE DREAM RIGHT

If to begin with the end in mind as a proactive way to live, titling chapters before writing them can guide the horse. The cart I wanted to carry with the title was a wishlist about my ideal lovestone, though then I thought about travel. Telling you three places I'd like and love to travel, all three are places I've already lived or visited; Hong Kong, Italy, and Australia.

If we have to choose between two things, sometimes we can do both, though that best not apply to mates or else it could be quite a mess. Blending ideas may cause confusion, yet I'm reminded again about the concept of immediate reality. I hold a moment within my comfort zone.

Canibus' track *Poet Laureate II* says: "I go with the given, you know what comes to me over the celestial wireless. Whenever it comes, you're lucky when you get it." Perhaps my girlfriend wants to tend the soil in which we grow? Roiling in waters and puddles of clay, instead of boiling the blood, she reminds me I'm like a cow to chew my cud.

The music I play seems to accuse me of being free. It's bizarre how some songs can speak direct references about our lives by artists who've never met us. Tracked voices can describe our exact situations precisely and manipulate what we think. It can seem like surgical implants communicate our thoughts.

Without being conscious of what we're doing, prerecorded lyrics seem to fuse preflexively. Comments more accurate than I can vocalize share truths holding and moulding my humble reverence. I was meant to be telling you about my desires as these Fountains are fantasy, yet there is faith in this too.

How and why could I ever want anything? I told one friend that it's okay to want things, though can I believe that for myself too? What is the dividing line between want, need, and greed? I remember not all wishes are for money, things or resources. There are other desires humans hold, such as peace, love, unity, and respect.

I'd love for my core family unit to expand beyond Zeus and me. When I wrote the chapter *Give In or Give Up*, it was about two or three months before this one. With the addition of three carefully placed blue towels, the contested clawing areas were guarded. The towels alleviate a great deal of anger and abuse by not needing to battle with Zeus and some of his power-control behaviours.

When I tell you I want to write my future into life, at times, I've been hesitant because I don't entirely know what I want. I want to sell books to earn money; that's true, yet it's an objective that needs me to market my work effectively. I've thought sharing free copies could expand my reach to readers, and it may, yet, how can I garner real live sales? Mass marketing isn't a core skill I possess, though I can learn skills.

I had just started Ramit Sethi's book *I'll Teach You to Be Rich*. Ramit's book excited and inspired me to pay off my debts. With online calculators, I found a $70 a month increase to my home loan can reduce the amortization by five years and lessen $10,000 of interest. To be debt-free, I must act appropriately and actively pay off my debts.

It was February 2019 when I started writing this Fountain. It's been a great year and experience to continue up to, and perhaps beyond, October with landscaping. From my earnings with Brad, I paid off $1,500 of my student loans by the close of July, and as soon as my student loans were paid, I started to think about fueling money into my savings and mortgage.

Earlier in the year, I wanted to get a car, though I have halted partly on the plan. I want to have a car again, though the lure of having $600-$800 discretionary money instead of a vehicle is tantalizing. I'd like more car friends who'll help out with lifts and accept gas money for rides, yet I loved it when people would chip in money for fuel when *I* was the car friend! We could jest about being a passenger or driver in life, yet I suppose that's better than being a crash test dummy.

So, three things I want; to be debt-free, to own a car, and to travel a bit (preferably with a travel buddy). I also want a girlfriend, yet I made a big rewind to the first Fountain. In *Finding Natalie,* I wrote about the real-girl/dream-girl/no-girl dilemma. Since I couldn't be with dream-girl, I wanted to find a real girl, yet as of now, I'm with no-girl.

I'm mostly okay being without a gal, and I've written about how I've learned to be alone. It is true Zeus is a pretty great companion, yet it's also true I'd like to have more female contact and more conversations. Solitary living is sometimes alright, being content is a good thing, yet I nudge forward for a bit more of what I want. It's a slow, gradual process. Bit by bit, grain by grain, and seed by seed, I heed my heart and soul becoming more aligned.

I've written a lot of audacious goals and objectives in the past, and they've not all manifested by the point of typing this. Some minor gains had acquiesced, and I wonder if it's my fear of acceptance hindering me. Is it my lack of faith, or a firm belief of scarcity or absence that's withheld forward motion? If I submit to the will of God and The Universe again, what shall flow out of the keys with ease to appease?

Why can we be so hesitant and unclear about saying what we want? Telling others what we desire is exceptionally valuable, especially if they can help us gain those things. Is it that I don't want what I want well enough to push for it? Sometimes I'm afraid of wanting things because I fear being considered greedy, yet wanting is a natural thing. Why have I put so many restrictions on myself and my core sets of desires? Precisely because I fear judgment.

With Providing Point, I was striving for meaning and purpose because I would have a significant function, yet I was thinking of providing for others from a purpose-driven motive. Instead of pure love, a humanitarian point of compassion and prerogative found me to push and expand for meaning.

I need to get outside of myself and what I want more

often, yet some online mentors and guides remind us the more we earn, the more we can give. Earn like the 1% and share 99%? Perhaps that's a great objective, yet if discussions of money are set aside, where does the mind wander?

If cares of the heart remind us of others loss and grief, is it best to not message them? If Heaven is a rightful place and the afterlife crosses over between the spirit and shadow realm, how may we glean further insight? If we cycle ahead four thousand days, is the home still where I want to reside?

Are free days working with the worth of the cross instead of the loss of paying to have a boss? In exchange for a gain of time and another late night, the power of love is strong enough to rewire the brain into understanding religious principles from an agnostic view. Who is it that wants me to spit out my food if I've not said a prayer for it?

Can I comprehend and share religious ideas without proclaiming them? I don't have a rock-solid faith. Why are there prayers in my books? Am I running away from God, bullishly refusing to catch the baton? I'm not sure of running His race because I don't want to dash into the afterlife. Who do I want to vote *onto* the island? We wind the threads of thought into a strong cord.

I pay homage while reminding myself such decisions are held out on a limb. Shimmying down to slimming down as a desire, the cigarettes met fire to stem the spire. Chemical pleasures are part of me and what I use to allow myself to retire, yet I halt to restructure. At this juncture, I pause to discover and amplify the cause.

If I'm meant to get the dream right, I remember some of the best dreams happen while we're awake. Perhaps agitation stems from processes that I've yet to comprehend, yet I want to not just have friends, yet also *be* a friend. I may need to reach out to some more often than they do to me as parts of this process stem from a seed to a tree.

Shards of My Soul was available at this point, and a feeling of accomplishment seeped into my being. It's weird because I've started to believe in my hopes, goals, and dreams.

Instinctively, I also must support future successes with action. I continue the Fountains past the ninth, and I intuit how to write and fuse enjoyment with the process of creating books.

It's a long task to write a book, and writing helps build positive faith resulting in good feelings. The experience of enduring through a long, arduous process has a satisfaction of its own, and while my dreamy side reminds me of only having rice to eat for thirty-nine days, an entirely different experience calls me to live as a non-smoker.

I've wanted to extend outwards from the Providing Point demographic to friends too. When I chose to give the 7th Fountain's earnings to friends, I imagined helping a lot of others with money, food, and other things. I believed the 7th Fountain would earn more than it had up to August 2019. The total royalties of Fountain seven at that point were $9.35.

Rings of Truth's committed cause is entirely in line with Zeus being here. When I wrote the section *Give In or Give Up*, it was not a safe home for Zeus back then, and I see how my work can be seen as penance. Each section can call me to repent and give and inspires me to share a due desire or influence. The 5th Fountains earnings going to Pencils of Promise, though that came from Lewis Howes and his podcast.

Reminders land in my email inbox, and though I don't want so many messages, I hold them aside to read. In the month I was in, Gabby Bernstein was a prominent mailer. Gabby's reminder is to do what feels good, and it couples with Christy Whitman's teachings to allow a manifestation of what is right. We must remember to amplify what's right for others, also in addition to what we like.

With ideas going back to my January 2018 trip, I know to not always do things purely on the premise that only others shall gain. I'm still learning, though I understand how I need to care for me first and *then* do the right things that benefit. I mustn't sacrifice myself to my own detriment as much as I used to.

Mentioning Gabby and Christy stem from my conscious

reminder of aligning with our best interests and core desires. After building foundations, we can construct our homes upon a reliable and sure base. I remember this and rethink some of what I've done before.

If I carry a real-estate metaphor, the first three three-part books were homes for my growth. I rent them out to others while changing how and where I'm living in the present moment. I need to get the dream right.

Visualizations and imagination are not always accessible, though, so if you have difficulty seeing in your mind what you want, write out what you want. Our dreams, fantasies, and realities change, yet remember that your life also may be like a glacier. Each wave of snowfall descends onto the mountains adding to what fell before, and the culmination is the fortified glacier of what your life now is. This can be both good or bad, so be careful what type of precipitation falls from your attitude.

Perhaps you don't like the cold and clouds, yet before our lives can become liquid water suitable to drink, sometimes a distillation process can help purify. Our past experiences and life on Earth hold cryptic debris deep under the layers of snow and ice, so tunnelling is an idea to dig further into the core. Journal entries are points to remind us, though, I'm not yet sure what I'm searching for.

I have a few thousand pages of written rhymes, yet I don't know if they are water or soil. If they are water, then we can use them to nourish the seeds, yet if they're soil, perhaps those preflexive seeds I mentioned earlier in the chapter can sprout.

Similar to my writing, my rhymes aren't clearly thought out or laid out with conscious intent. Like my books, there are shards and fragments of ideas and the work seems to be controlled by forces that aren't me. When my music plays, I didn't have a conscious awareness of intent about how it's heard.

When music sites ask me to share similar artists, I don't even know who to say. I can tell you who's influenced me, who I've played on CD or mp3, yet I can't compare myself to others. I don't want to get mixed up in egos and attitudes that conflict, so where I seem to put myself is a solitary nodal point or as a person of random interest. I call my music genre Introversial.

Unlike many people seeking to be famous or garner massive amounts of attention, I'm really quite thankful for my kind, peaceful, and boring life, and though I'm not seeking fame, my actions seem to contradict. If I'm putting books, YouTube tracks, CDs, or emails out to the world, what am I searching for? You know, I don't know.

This may go back to how I'm a sea-dwelling creature, just climbing out and about putting on showy behaviour. I'm not the best or better, I'm just doing what I do while often neglecting or not being aware of the consequences.

Perhaps as we learn what the intrinsically right things for us are, we can fortify peace, develop love, and share respect in and with full unity.

20/20 VISION

Remember what you have accomplished, and recall the comments others have made reminding you of your process. Sit and hold a breath telling yourself to move forward with people supporting your efforts.

My friend Bert told me he thinks the keyword of my work is 'growth' yet I've been resisting acceptance that my work has meaning and value. The saying "I still don't know" is one I've fused into Fountains often. Initially, the motif was about Natalie and how I still don't know her, though perhaps the shift is also how I've not yet known success with the Fountains.

Much has been gained, though. This section of the book is self-therapy to tell myself of my positive bits and acknowledge some of what I've learned by writing the Fountains.

I may not have found Natalie, yet the journey is extensive. I started writing the first book about six years ago, and it took two to three years to finish that first manuscript. The quality of *Finding Natalie* is awful compared to recent releases, and I've learned how to craft a quality book. My obscure ramblings and nattering still lace the pages I form, yet too, a developing eloquence fortifies.

I've often focused on money and earnings instead of people, and in the past half-year, I've not had as much lack as in the previous years. At some points in this writing journey, I've mentioned scraping the wastebasket for shreds of tobacco to smoke. I've been a smoker, yet having part-time work freed up my concern about having enough to puff.

I've written about needing to find alternate sources of income other than my writing, and, with a job, I have. I've also written about how I need to focus more on people and develop and entrust real friendships with people. I do.

I've grown a lot since starting these books, yet my assuaged notions of self-disdain and worthlessness also taint my heart. She calls out to me through my soul, yet it seems I must refute any wishes I've had before connecting.

It's been twenty-one years since a song trained my being how to love according to my delusions, and now I must re-circuit my authentic pathways back onto what is real. I've been living with desires of fantasy for decades when I should've been focused on truth.

How do we reach the Fountains of Flourishing? They may be two or so years away from now, yet are those three Fountains to process the fantasies I've held onto into the real channels of who I am and what I want?

Can clarity hone what shall be into homes that manifest? For a couple years, I was quite religious and wrote chapters about God, Jesus, and Heaven. In recent weeks and months, I've still prayed, yet not as often as I had when I held a stronger belief.

My faith in God has shifted with trust in the Universe and fate and also extricates myself from false worship. I have sometimes felt guilt or fear by not praying before eating food, and in real moments of gratitude, I say thank you in different languages.

My reverence for God is there, yet I'm not clear about recognition. I've barely ever heard the voice or intuition of God, and want to know what is real and not blindly throw thanks at Him if I don't know who He is.

While writing before, I've mentioned how I was told literally every letter, space, and period was formed without my choice; an entire predestined sequence of words and punctuation. Other people tell us we have free-will and opportunity; that we can do whatever we want to whenever we want to.

Sometimes when I become aware I have the chance to speak, I can't articulate a single word from my mouth. I've claimed my meds prevent me from communicating, and my medication does affect me. Sometimes it feels like I'm entirely under control by forces I can't pinpoint.

Sounds from the world outside of my home bark in fears; seemingly to disrupt my flow of thought and change my pathway. If I try to exert my desires and will into the text and choose my actions, it seems stifling ideas keep me from being myself.

I very well could write on the question "who am I" and not be able to answer accurately. I know my name. I also could tell you what I've said or written. Yet the central core of who I am may not entirely be definable. Nouns could label me, adjectives could attempt to describe, yet the actions of what I sometimes do and say also could paint a dreary story.

I've sought to have value instead of understanding the parts of me that are valuable. I have put in time and energy into the Fountains and seeded the first few patrons, yet one other helpful thing about me and my work is I follow through with my promises.

We've not housed the first person yet, though I also follow through with the earnings distributions I've written about. My books have generated (up to October 8th, 2019) $291.72 for charity, and if you're reading this book, more is shared from sales after this release.

My inner and external dilemmas come from committing to work for others while also wanting to earn for me. A difficulty I face is wanting to give more than I spend while also finding ways to make more.

The idea of the secondary gains for myself seems to suggest I think of others first. Cognitively that's partly true, as I'm often aware of outer parts of life, yet more truly I'm neurotically wrapped up in my own thoughts and challenges.

The biggest challenge I've faced is bullishly and dismissively committing to Providing Point while not feeling thrilled to do so. I want to naturally gather and generate prosperity, yet I lack the genuine care and passion for getting onto the street to actively help people. I want an abundant life, yet I also want others to have abundant experiences too.

I work landscaping, and even if I like my boss and I can earn some money for him by being an employee, I also want the freedom, finances, and space to passively work on anything I want to. This goes back to working for others. By working for my boss, I earn money, yet the wish is I could sell something (even if not my books) so that I can afford to live with irregular sleep patterns. I don't like waking up early and feel far more inclined to work on the computer at night.

The dilemma of working alone at night is a separate issue when wanting to be well integrated into life. Perhaps parts of the Providing Point idea are right, and my books may still house people. Not so many books have sold up to October 2019, though that's a reason why the Patreon page is used to gather.

I can't shake the idea that I need to provide for others and not only myself. Earnings from my job are seemingly selfish earnings, while book sales are a sign I am doing the right things on Earth. I seem to have a belief that links financial rewards with just actions.

"The right thing, at the right time, for the right reason."-Owen Beattie

I'm a friend, employee, community member, son, and nephew. I'm also a human, a writer, and a lost soul. I'm a person who attempts to be profound, while I also link rhymes on the Internet as MindSound. I have received support from the government, and it's valued, required, and helpful, though the audacious wishes include earning the entirety of my income from work, books, music, and providing.

My home is a place where I almost seem imprisoned with my mind tethered to obsessive tendencies and devious devices. Entranced by stillness and the aghast fears of consequence for being who I am, the keys seize moments of incepted thought and etch them upon stone and time.

I value solitude, it helps with productivity, yet I also appreciate people and relationships. How many friends do I even have, though? Have I been trying to buy my way in life?

I'd love to choose to share and buy things for people, yet have I been trying to lord over people by offering crumbs?

Is Providing Point a waste of time? How much benefit is $15 a month to someone? For those who have less, a little bit means a lot, yet what can I give to people that have more? I can give my time to those with money, yet want to use my money with some to save 'time'?

And yet the breeze on my deck as I typed this remind me I'm wealthy. Some have cars and more income than I do and are still financially concerned. Some of them also have relationship issues and mouths to feed while I wish I could have a lovestone to live and build with.

My cat is fantastic, and I have an apartment to live in. I even have had the chance to write so much up to now and develop my skills and abilities. I have time to read books and learn, and I have the desire that others may also thrive. I don't want others to be poor.

I don't want to be above people either, even if it's nice to live on the top floor. When I throw a prayer up and out, it's sometimes to the ceiling or out to the sky where satellites could be recording the very moment and place I sit or stand.

I abhor evil, deceit, and wickedness, yet smoke the foul, filthy cigarettes that are a vice of my creative freedom. Having a tin of tobacco to me is a sign of prosperity and is a pleasure I don't often want to sacrifice.

Yet my health is poor. I can't run very far. I have a bit of a fat belly. My teeth are yellow. I don't eat regularly. I love to drink coffee and Coke. I've also neglected to exercise.

I used to go to Tae Kwon Do and recall how much fitter I was back then. Even if I was a smoker back then, I was stronger, more flexible, and my behaviours and thoughts were far more disciplined.

And yet now, I've become more self-aware, I've developed my ability to write, and I've started to think, perhaps obsessively, about what I can contribute. My conscientious nature fortifies a stubborn resolve to ignore what others tell me I *should* do while I, instead, focus on doing what I want to do.

Having a job is an excellent source of money, though earning hinged upon required labour compares to desired work. I wish to win through creative effort. The books and gathering entwine so tightly, though what would happen if I rewound back to the first book? If I never thought of giving from the earnings, what would have I written?

The release of the first book was not fueled by charitable motives. I don't think, back then, that I even believed Natalie would ever read a copy. I know now that the 49% royalty lure is a motivation for me, and if I go back to the 1st and 2nd Fountain, I recall I wanted to earn money back then too.

What was the twist in the 4th Fountain that called me along the dismal darkened pathway to seemingly nothing for anything? Why do I keep pressing the keys in the 10th, and if I want to share valuable text to readers, why haven't I?

The Freedom Solution cues again. To do what we want to do, with whom we want to do it when we want to do it, where we want to do it, and with full financial support.

Let's check the self/other parameters of the Freedom Solution. For others first, please; what do people want to do? I don't know, I've barely asked. It's a great question to ask someone: "What do you want to do?" Often we get the response, "I don't know, what do you want to do?" Perhaps people like me need to more clearly think about what they want to do. After we find out what we want to do, others can help us find what we want.

When I think of things I want, I think of having a car. I also think the core desire is more so *being* things. I want to *be* a loved, trusted, and appreciated friend, I want to *be* free to choose how and when to go to sleep, and I want to *be* at home with my lovestone and be able to talk with her. I want to have a home where I can turn around and talk to someone and have them talk back to me.

I think my Freedom Solution is basic. I want to live with a girlfriend and insanely and obsessively work on my creative projects while knowing I have a real true love whom I can talk with, who also lives with Zeus. Sometimes, I do like my life now. When I typed this, I was in line with my truths and had the luxuries of coffee, lates night to work, cigarettes, and a kind reminder that life is a lot better when I live with someone.

"Like the deserts miss the rain" - *Everything But the Girl*

Yet, ironically, the lyric holds much more substance to a different love. I've sometimes thought of the lyric and how deep sadness can permeate when I think I'll never meet the one I really love. I feel like a desert wishing for rain, yet not like one that's known if before.

I feel sad, devoid, and solemn, knowing I don't have a girlfriend, no matter how many other beautiful things I have. Zeus is great, yet I want to find *my* mate and live with her too. Who is she, though?

QUALITY IS OUR RECIPE

This section is a girlfriend wishlist. Where shall I start with my wishlist? It's telling what the first item someone says is; yet in writing, it's even trickier because it's there for all readers to see and assess.

If I'm to hook up with a gal, first, she must be single when we do so. She must accept that I'm, for now, a smoker and not expect me to quit. I may stop, yet I've no idea as to when. I also hope she forgives me for all the apostrophes on the page. If we have a kid, I don't want to have written so many contractions into her life from my attempt to be concise.

Do we have kids? Not necessarily. I led the 4th Fountain with a chapter written to Aeris, a potential future daughter, yet it's not a requirement my gal births our child. Physiologically, I may not be able to have kids, and adoption isn't off the table. I'm partly ambivalent about being a Dad to a real live human and am not sure if my next girlfriend needs to be childfree.

My financial situation shows I don' know how to afford to cover more than my own and Zeus' lives. For things I like to do, I like going out to dinner and movies, I love walks and conversation, and for a bonus point, I enjoy snuggling. My gal may need to be a cuddly person and also best give real full-on hugs. I'm physically affectionate with some and want to have a secure physical connection with a gal; not so much sex, though that's bonus points.

Regarding trust and truth, I want her to feel comfortable to tell me her honest opinions without concern about upsetting me or setting me off. I value radical honesty, though that doesn't mean not having tact and being kind. I can be a bit abrupt, so I remember I may need an understanding and accepting gal.

I don't have a car yet, so it'd be rad if she does, or we can share and go halfers on one. As I like having money, it'd be great if she has a job or career and understand how to discuss finances. From Ramit Sethi's book *I Will Teach You to Be Rich*, I learned a few intriguing things about money recently, so it'd be awesome she reads that book too. My gal doesn't need to be an avid reader, and I'm not clear how I'll respond if she's a bookworm.

My gal doesn't need to have a post-secondary education, though that would be a plus. I like women who're smart and can talk a lot, yet also value questions and hope she's inquisitive. Sometimes I need to have a cue to get me started, yet there's also a delicate line about being an interrogator and asking too many questions. Oppositely, it's rad to have a gal who knows how to speak while also not overloading me with too much. Communication skills are necessary.

My girlfriend has a fantastic sense of humour. I'm not sure if it's dark, yet there must be a potential edge for rudeness and puns are often welcome. She must be ready for reruns of my jokes and not-so-random repeats as I like long-running threads of inside jokes as shared humour. I'll obviously tell her jokes that are in poor taste, yet she'll know I am generally not biased, and I know some things should not be joked about, period.

Another critical thing about my girlfriend is that she'll want to meet my other friends. I want to form a merging or sharing of friends and meet hers too because I like how when friends meet each other, tactical information can be gleaned. I'd like that my girlfriend can speak of tactics and schemes without being manipulative or malicious, yet a different way of saying that is that she's smart and wise and can help me with my blind spots with other people.

Regarding being a drinker, she doesn't need to drink alcohol, yet having a glass of wine leads to a communication exercise I like. A game of twenty-questions could play out, though one thing at a time. For drinking, it's okay for her to drink rarely or occasionally, though absolutely not a habit beyond one glass a day. Even a glass a day is a bit much, yet I'd prefer maybe one or two drinks per week outside of meals.

From meals, we go to the Glass House to compound the text. The island in our kitchen (if she and I do build the home) is a place where we can prepare meals and also chat with our friends while we make food. She doesn't need to be a great cook at this point, yet she best have a willingness to learn and work with me in the kitchen. I'd like to make sure she's open to talking about cooking sessions and meal preparation, even if my current home is limited.

If we build the Glass House, part of the vision is to hold gatherings there to earn and pay for the home. If we can expand and grow to the point of having meetings in that home, I wonder how she and I can work together on projects. We'll need excellent communication skills and also knowledge and the ability to listen, guide, and create. I don't know how artistic she needs to be, yet I like people who paint, draw, sing, dance, or write. Business, too, is an art.

Walks are a must. Not for our dog, though. I don't want to own a dog at this point in my life. In the future, perhaps, yet not while I'm living in an apartment. Maybe she has a dog, though we'd need to have two homes to allow that at this point in the journey. I live in an apartment and won't live with a dog while I'm here. How will the first years of her and I's relationship develop? We've yet to see. I wonder what she'd think of two Calico kittens?

I remind myself that I've talked about living together, yet haven't so much talked about marriage. I'm not entirely afraid of such, yet one thing at a time.

An idea I've shared is the half-the-age-plus-seven rule. If older, divide your age by two and add seven. E.g. I'm forty-one. Twenty and a half plus seven is twenty-seven and a half; my lower bracket. I would have skipped this rule with one gal (she's twenty-six), though she chose another for now.

Religion? She's hopefully not evangelical Christian. I like those who are open to talking about spiritual matters, and

I'd like to further develop my understanding and exploration of belief, but I don't want to be preached at, even if she believes. She hopefully is respectful and open to learning about other religions, and I'll dig it if she's into meditation. I want to develop my spiritual understanding and exploration and could use some shared support.

With podcasts, I hope we can play and hear them and also talk about what we've heard. Talking about ideas and concepts that aren't part of the everyday conversation are radially good and stimulate new connections. The activity of laying down on couches and just talking or letting a podcast or music play is enjoyable for relaxation.

I'd love for her to be entirely open to talking about money and finances too. My earnings aren't great, though it'd be stellar to have a gal who's into long-term planning and also wise with her money. This doesn't mean that she doesn't spend on herself or some luxuries, though that she and I can talk about our earnings and form a conscious spending plan we can share. When we move in together, it'll be awesome to discuss and plan our financial future together.

She also must be compassionate and forgiving. A different way of saying that is that she must have a kind heart and be empathetic. Not so much for me, yet also for the wellbeing of others. She must be okay with Zeus if we're to live together, and oppositely, Zeus shall help guide me to know she's the right one.

Family is the entire group of people living together, and a home is where that family may live and thrive. I've known some gals who don't have great relationships with their parents, yet are still thoroughly decent people. In a previous part of this journey, I wrote how I want my gal to be on good terms with her family. It's ideal, yet not an absolute necessity.

What might be a necessity, though, is that she gets along with my family. I'd love to go to Australia with her and visit Dad and Sarah and have them thoroughly happy and thankful that my gal is brought along. If we need to pay for the trip, that links back to money and planing to afford trips together.

From the word 'trips,' I think she shouldn't do drugs because I don't want to be in a home where drugs are beyond the catnip for Zeus and my coffee and ciggies. I mentioned how I want her to be okay with me smoking, yet I'm twisted up and in about whether or not I'd be okay with her smoking. If we both smoke, then that could be a life-long entrapment with nicotine instead of me finding the desire to quit and live a longer life with her.

It's difficult living alone for so many years. I want to gain the experience and skills needed to live with a gal full-time and believe the best way to do so is by doing so. I don't want to go out looking for love in all the wrong places, yet how am I to find a gal who wants to live with me if I'm at home alone?

Some have recommended Internet sites like Plenty-of-Fish, and though I don't know who I'll live with beyond Zeus, I remind myself she won't magically fall from the sky. I'm not as soul-bound with Natalie like I thought I was, and I also got hooked up on Elspeth and reacted negatively when I couldn't connect with her.

Chandra is terrific, yet I'm not clear about living with her full-time. Of the gals I do know, there are barely any I'd love to be in full-contact with. I also don't want to 'pick' one because I more so want to be the one chosen. I want my gal to want me and seek out a relationship with me and then receive her.

Fear of rejection is a legitimate cop-out for me, though, differently, I've let gals know I like them a lot, and then they don't want to connect. I've had massive crushes on gals, which I know isn't healthy, yet my wishes and dreams for a lovestone may be a good sign.

It'd be cool for her to read my books and be interested in forming a relationship. That's the tactic I started with about Natalie in the first book, though my obsessive nature and the intentional selection was for one I don't know and one who theoretically didn't want me.

I'd love to be in love, and I'd like to know what she likes.

I want her to want to connect and make an effort to do so. I also wish someone could wish upon a star and tell me exactly who you are.

Two decades of being solo have worn on me, and I don't see a quick fix for it either. I've said often it feels like I'm at the start, and it seems like my love hasn't yet begun. Two decades ago, I thought I knew who I'd live with and have kids, yet I've not seen her in real life. I want to build *with* someone and not construct impossible fantasies. That means that the highest probability and best situation is to find a gal who wants to make a life with me.

I refuse to believe that the world has been conspiring for me to bring the lovestone into my awareness. Coleman had asked, "what if there's a gal that thinks of you the way you thought of Natalie?" Perhaps, similarly, if there is, I'd love for her to let me know who she is. Differently, Natalie has thousands of fans that love her and would like to meet, while I seem to be alone wondering if anyone would like to connect.

I'm quite glad I don't have thousands of screaming fans, though it'll be rad to find my biggest fan as one I'd love to live with too. I don't know when you'll read this book, though it may be a precursor for you to read the others to look into what I've shared. Even if I dream, I still think my rational limitations override my desires.

I want to go to the islands and dance in the sand; hand in hand with a look deep into her eyes, reminding me she thinks I'm her prize. Wanting and wishing for love is a solitary activity. Doing so requires a fixation, yet a real relationship is an active engagement of two's spirit and their soul.

I've thought often that destiny and fate were making me wait. Perhaps I waited too long? Maybe I should have gone across the oceans to find her before settling into writing a book. I've written about acceptance a bit and how it's valuable, yet I've also written that wanting things is okay too.

If we have a desire, we often attempt to find a way to satiate that want. What if I've wanted too much and haven't had the gumption to work for it? What if I've worked on these books pushing for prosperity instead of finding ways to live in genuine love? If I want to provide and share love, why didn't I advocate for her to be my love in real life?

Has my self-focused nature removed the beautiful parts of myself she used to like? Would she like to be my mate and not just a friend? If I told her how I felt, is she afraid to reciprocate? Does she want me, yet found me focused on a different gal? Is she afraid to reach out to me because I told her too much?

Had I not known that love is how we always are, are we separated by universes, a galaxy, and a star? If I've told her I love, is that something she can't sense as real no matter what I feel? Or, perhaps, she feels unwanted and doesn't get I want to live with her and our pet.

If there is one bit of advice laced in this text, it's to tell people how you feel and what you mean. Not being able to speak to someone doesn't mean you don't like them or don't want to be with them. There may be other reasons they don't return your calls or texts.

I still don't know.

Though what if this is a couple decades later and you met me. I hope you've read the books and have seen all of my lost hopes, goals, and dreams and still chose to forgive me for not knowing what to say. Just because I have piles of love to sieve before I give, I also feel devoid of positive characteristics. I hope you looked into my flaws and found acceptance.

I still may get obsessive and overbearing, though I'll try to be the best human I can be for you. Love is real, and note this time it's not capitalized. You're a beautiful human and soul, and even if I didn't know where to enroll in your life yet, thank you for being patient and letting me come to know our truth. Youth seems so close and far away, yet rewind back to *Life is a Sunset;* "forever and a day."

SUBTLE DISTINCTION

To go a bit meta, I'd like to share with you the process of how the individual Fountains form. Before writing the individual books, I've often had a clear idea about what I want the book to be, yet the books barely ever result in how I intended.

I don't write outlines for these books, and often the natural course of events and thoughts show the meandering formations of text. In some Fountains, I've input timestamps in sections to share where I was when I was writing their first draft; temporal points are helpful with an evolving process.

Each Fountain is eleven to thirteen chapters long. The length of the books comes from the format of the first three. For *Finding Natalie* through to *Fields of Formation*, I printed the books in sixty to seventy page eight by eleven magazine-sized forms. It was *A Distant Glimmer* (the 6th Fountain) when I chose to adjust the books to 5.5"x8.5" sizing. I went back to *Seeds of Tomorrow* and *Fields of Formation* and rereleased them the same.

Even now, though, I write the individual books in the 8½"x 11" format for their first draft. Each chapter is usually titled before I start writing the sections to give me guidance about what I'm writing about. Each block of text is almost always five lines of 12 point Book Antiqua text with a neurotic tendency to have each line cover all the way to the right side of an unjustified page. It's rare that I even add even one word extra to start a sixth line; maybe less than 5% of the time.

I'll write the five-line blocks and attempt to open the next bit with a separate thought that doesn't follow the previous one; basic paragraphing, yet to the five-line format. Sometimes the text blurs, though I attempt to carry the thread of one block into a followable series.

I strive for conciseness by adjusting the words I use as I learn how to write better, and I've improved my writing a lot since the first few Fountains. It was in *Fields of Formation*'s revision where I started to level up in editing, though improved even further later with Grammarly significantly enhancing my work.

The objective is to complete chapters in one sitting, though that doesn't always happen. The chosen title gives me guidance, and as I start to write, I draw out the text in the five-line paragraphs. I add or subtract ideas to keep in these blocks as best I can, though sometimes I find myself out of words or ideas for a chapter. In those cases, I'll just stop typing and not force the process. In other instances, I push and strive to keep the cursor slugging across the page and down the lines to push forward to completion.

A chapter is 'done' when I've written about four and a half pages of text. When I complete the thoughts for a section, I'll often have an inspiration for what the next chapter is going to be and write the title for the next chapter.

Not always, though often, I can return to the Fountain with a line of awareness about where I want to guide the streams of text. If I don't finish a chapter in one sitting, I'll come back to the Word document, reread what I've written, and then continue.

Titling the books is one way I heed subconscious guidance too. Almost always, I know what the next book's title is. I didn't have that with *Rings of Truth*, yet for the first three three-part books, I knew most of the titles before they were released. The titles of the first three three-part books all include particulate ideas; *Fragments of Intent*, *The Sands of Yesterday*, and *Shards of My Soul*. This is by accident, yet it shows how I know I'm a bit scatterbrained and not whole.

After I'm done writing a chapter, I'll often run a Grammarly check on the text after it's written to help for later revision. I don't do rewriting at that stage, though a Grammarly clean up helps the book when it comes time to rewrite and revise.

After the eleven to thirteen base chapters are done (the goal of 65 pages of base text), I copy and paste the sections into the 5 ½"x8 ½" book template. I then change all of the text to 12 point Garamond font. Since the pages are smaller than the first drafts format, chapters extend in page length, though the writing is still in the chunked blocks. After sorting out the Garamond shift and blocking to the template of a smaller book size, then we get to the tricky part, Revision.

If writing a book isn't so easy, and you want to be an author, get ready for your soul to be ripped through its own self if you're going to create the final version. Revision, I find, can be crucially tricky, though the revision and rewriting are becoming a quicker process now that I've learned a bunch.

Although, at the point of not being a professional editor, it's beneficial to clean up and prepare. I've never had any of my work edited by another person, and I don't follow many rules, though I've hopefully have crafted some decent books. I don't know how the quality of my finished works compare to others, yet I do and don't care. I'm creating what I want to develop and absolve obligations of catering to what *'should'* be done.

That said, some things *need* to be done to write a book. Rewriting and revision are necessary. First, I start at the beginning and see how it reads. I read each line and adjust the text to how I want it to read, and I make sure that what I'm saying reads as I want to say it. I attempt to carry a cadence and flow of words, yet since I have the initial blocks (the five lines per paragraph in the draft), I start to segment each line into formed sections.

If an idea stops short, or it reads into the next links of a text block, I edit and form naturally sounding segments. My paragraph formation occurs with the text revision as I slowly reshape the initial chapter. I adust sentence structure and revise the book chapter by chapter until I like how it reads. It takes me only an hour or so to edit a section.

When I get stressed out, pissed off, tired, or think I'm creating garbage, I'll stop. Just as how it's difficult to be likable when we're pissed off, creating requires patient care for good work. After I rewrite and reform the paragraphs into a cohesive text, I'll Grammarly the document again. After Grammarly, I'll go back and reread, making changes as a digital proofread.

By this point, it's been about two to four digital passes, and I'll start to think I'm getting there. If I believe the entire book reads well, I'll go online with KDP (Kindle Direct Publishing) and start setting up the release. KDP is the channel I used for publishing, though this is about my process, not quite publishing.

The goal of my revision process is to read an Unlimited Version of a book. The Unlimted version is a version of the book that I feel good about, enough to soon release. I've often ordered copies of the books and have made them available on Amazon when in Unlimited form, yet they're not the final version.

The first Unlimited Fountains were Fountains four and five. I've been using that format since. After a Fountain is in Unlimited Form, I order proofs, yet at this point, the book still isn't done.

After a full reread and manual revision of the book – making sure it reads well and adjusting the style and flow with punctuation – I then have to transcribe the manual edits into the digital file.

Once the transcription is done, another run of Grammarly and I think I've got a finished book! Nope... not yet. One more proof (or release copy) of the post-Unlimited version is brought in for another manual proofread sometimes. After transcribing edits and a final Grammarly run, we have a single Fountain's completion.

One by one, the individual books form and still won't always be the best they can be. I make them better and better with each revision, though when the Fountains are done, it's later time to bundle them. Putting the three-parters together has been a bit different for each. With *Fragments of Intents*, I cut about thirteen or so chapters from the final release. The book is just fragments of the first three books.

The Sands of Yesterday was better, and the difference in writing style and ability is significant. For Sands, the three post-Unlimited books were formatted together and went through another two manual revisions and digital updates. I don't feel completely confident in that book, though. It's highly probable my lack of confidence in that book is why I didn't market or push it so much. I was writing to earn at that point, even if I'd promised away most of the earnings.

Shards of My Soul is the first book I feel confident I created something worthwhile to read. What I lacked in that book was clarity as to *why* I was writing and also *what* I was writing. I continued the process by following from the energy of the 7th Fountain, which was impelled partly by writing for writing. Even though I've learned how to write better, the push to continue found it unfocused.

The process for how the text of these books forms can channel from a flawed foundation. I'm still building, yet I'm not sure *Rings of Truth* is entirely rational and cohesive either. I need to focus, structure and hone a complete book. Perhaps the 11th shall be different, and if ten, eleven, and twelve melds into their three-parter, maybe I can show how we can build successfully on a flawed foundation, even if not recommended.

This was meant to be the second last chapter in *Rings of Truth*, though impatience can lead to adjusted intents. As this shifted along the shoreline, the book may not make a huge difference, yet I guess if I'm not selling thousands, how can the individual Fountains earn for others?

It's not rational to believe there will be many individual Fountain's sales, yet if *Shards of My Soul* reaches a broader audience, perhaps Fountains ten and beyond can be significant earners. The idea is right, at least I wish and hope.

On CharityNavigator.org, I searched for charities and found some things. For leaders of the charities, almost all were earning six-figure salaries. I understand people should receive compensation for running organizations, yet when the benefit is over 10% of the total gathered, that makes me feel a bit nauseous.

I'm hesitant to declare or decree earnings from future books when they're not done, though keep an idea in mind for the next. An instinct to push on and create hounds me repeatedly as a perceived need, and I understand it's not *me* providing for people; it's an urge and responsibility I wish not to denounce.

If the saying is "finish what you started," then I *must* hold firm and do something to activate the ideas of previous Fountains. I can't force a seed to grow, though are the fountains the water the seeds need for hope and faith? Have the tendrils started to grasp at the world and not just my soul?

These concepts and ideas are still in their potential phase, and I hope they become fruitful. As I need a bit of guidance and form, if we can sprout the seeds and tend them well, perhaps our gardens and fields may flourish.

The metaphor is beans growing without lattice; they could sprawl and not bear fruit if they don't have support. They also could climb other trees and entwine with the other branches, so having a structure to work with and grow on may aid in a productive and reliable harvest of seeds.

I need to break and breathe a bit to reaffix my mind, my heart, and my soul into alignment. I realize adding more could make things complex, and even if I'm a pretty simple person, sometimes I confuse things with too much input and random ideas.

With the Fountains, the pages of text can be simplified; find what you like and love, make some solid and positive promises, and then work and follow through to achieve and honour them.

What's the next step and next book? The next Fountain is titled *Depths of Discovery* and is the second Fountain in the Fountains of Fantasy. *Signs of Serenity*, the 12th, forms concurrently with the 11th and compiles to *Mosaic of Miracles*.

Are there things you want to do or make that you've not drawn yourself to do or create? Are you thinking about releasing a book? An album? Would you like to find ways of earning more time or money?

Are you trying to find a balance between different situations or people? Are you wanting to start from scratch in a new home or form a new relationship? Are you just content to be and drift into the next waves of consciousness?

What would you like to learn? Are you a reader for escape or enjoyment? Have you cleared any of your issues? Do you just want to live, love, and thrive?

There is, for some, an urge or need to create. Being playful can be great for us, and, if we cultivate our mindstates, we also can find more ways to say and pray. Demonstrating values and ethics in action can share spirit and heart with the world in ways we cannot yet imagine.

After the next two books, we meet the Fountains of Flourishing. This book was dramatically more challenging to write for the first draft and easier for editing. When I was up to here in the first draft, I thought I was going to have to rehash, relive, and dredge a ton of bad feelings out of myself to rewrite it. It seemed like I'd never finish the release of *Rings of Truth*, yet if the 11th and 12th Fountains manifest into their three-part book, this may seem like a cakewalk.

I believe in growth and strength through difficulty, though I don't want to call against myself forces of any sort. By asserting some of what I have written, said, and told, I must level up and transform my wishes into reality.

I build my faith upon consecrated layers and tests of truth while also allowing myself to siphon pretty rad ideas and secrets into mirth. By living through what I've been through, I've gained some experience through fortuitous circumstances, yet if chance, fate, and destiny are the twine upon which the vines grab hold, be cautious which threads you follow.

Just because someone is leading doesn't mean we should follow them. Just because we follow, it doesn't mean we're not also guiding. If we can level the field and approach each other respectfully, with compassion, and without being deceived, then hopefully common grounds of decency can help let us know who to trust, and what the truth is.

If our homes can be studios as well as apartments or houses, Housing First philosophies are congruent with my understanding. If I didn't have a home to live in, I'd have zero chance of working on books *or* having a place to sleep or keep my cat or food.

Here's something else to think of:

"The States Parties to the present Covenant recognize the right of everyone to an adequate standard of living for himself and his family, including adequate food, clothing and housing, and to the continuous improvement of living conditions" - Article 11, International Covenant on Economic, Social and Cultural Rights

With the unstable emotions and feelings I've had with my cat, I had thought I could get back to working for Providing Point and books if he moved out. I also see, now, that if I can give and keep an excellent home for Zeus, that I can do both; I can provide a loving home for Zeus and myself and also get back to the plow in the communal fields.

As much as I've said and done, I've been playing in the mud and hadn't looked into the clouds recently. I've not done much to provide homes for people, and I recognize it's not just compassionate to want people to have homes, it is part of an international covenant.

The previous mayor of Chilliwack said it's the responsibility of the province to assist with the homeless population, though I'm inclined to think it's the responsibility of each member of the community *and* that *I've* not done enough. Maybe it is time to dig deeper and dive into *Depths of Discovery?*

CLOSING NOTES FOR RINGS OF TRUTH

This book formed with more ease and difficulty than previous Fountains. The first draft developed between February 2019 and August 2019 with some complicated feelings and energy. The revision process, though, seemed much more straightforward. I don't know if it's entirely due to skill and honing my production process.

100% of this book's earnings go to the Chilliwack Animal Safe Haven. I used to volunteer there and know it's a beautiful home for cats who need shelter. During the chapter Give In or Give Up, I was sure that's where Zeus was going to go. As of October 2019, Zeus still lives in my home, and I'm massively thankful I didn't give him the boot.

I also want to resurface more of my positive past. It's a therapeutic process and valuable to remember more of the good times. The Fountains have been like processing journals, yet focused on my wishful future and reporting my thoughts, not telling you my stories and history. Perhaps a moving memoir is an idea. That said, who'd want to read.

Thank you very much for reading this book. I send you each huge wishes of love, luck, and life. Please allow yourselves to thrive, and I hope you may learn, share, and gather more.

Peace, Love, Unity, and Respect

Robert

Other Book and Links

--

Shared Node (Key to Me)

Shared Node is a book of flowetics and rhymes by Rob and The Contialis.
(To release late 2019 or early 2020)

--

Seeds of Tomorrow (the 4th Fountain)
Fields of Formation (the 5th Fountain)
A Distant Glimmer (the 6th Fountain)
Etched in Stone (the 7th Fountain)
Open to Fate (the 8th Fountain)
Sand to Silt (the 9th Fountain)
Rings of Truth (the 10th Fountain)

--

Fragments of Intent - From the First Three Fountains

51% of Fragments of Intent's earnings go to Ann Davis Transition
Society

The Sands of Yesterday (The Second Three Fountains)

A compilation of the 4th, 5th, and 6th Fountain books.
51% of The Sands of Yesterday's earnings go to Providing Point

Shards of My Soul (The Fountains of Fortitude)

A compilation of the 7th, 8th, and 9th Fountain books.
51% of Shards of My Soul's earnings go to Cyrus Center, a group that
tends to at-risk youth

--

www.Patreon.com/Introversial to provide for those in need.

--

www.Patreon.com/RobertKoyich to give to Rob's creative
income in exchange for PDFs and mp3s.

--

To email Rob, message **Robert@RobertKoyich.com**

--

RobertKoyich.com

Made in the USA
Lexington, KY
07 November 2019

56723056R00061